In Step

With Fashion

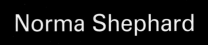
200 years of shoe style

WITHDRAWN

Norma Shephard

Schiffer Publishing Ltd®

4880 Lower Valley Road Atglen, Pennsylvania 19310

FOR JIM

This shoe image was used to advertise the Miss Priss Boutique in Belleville, ON.

Other Schiffer Books by Norma Shephard:
Lingerie: Two Centuries of Luscious Design
    ISBN: 0-7643-2818-3 $29.95
1000 Hats ISBN:0-7643-2403-9 $39.95
Accessorizing the Bride ISBN: 0-7643-2185-4 $49.95

Designed by "Sue"
Type set in Garton/Zurich BT
ISBN: 978-0-7643-2817-6   Printed in China

Value Guide: The price of vintage shoes varies widely and does not always reflect their condition, but often their historic importance. Autographed shoes from renowned ballerinas, for example, fetch very high prices. For the purposes of this book, shoes shown are appraised according to their condition, workmanship, style, rarity, fabrication, wearability, designer, and provenance (if known). It is assumed that prices given apply to purchases made at highest retail level and reflect the current marketplace. Values with the captions are given for vintage and antique the items only.

Published by Schiffer Publishing Ltd.
4880 Lower Valley Road
Atglen, PA 19310
Phone: (610) 593-1777; Fax: (610) 593-2002
E-mail: Info@schifferbooks.com

For the largest selection of fine reference books on this and related subjects, please visit our web site at
www.schifferbooks.com
We are always looking for people to write books on new and related subjects. If you have an idea for a book please contact us at the above address.

This book may be purchased from the publisher.
Include $5.00 for shipping.
Please try your bookstore first.
You may write for a free catalog.

In Europe, Schiffer books are distributed by
Bushwood Books
6 Marksbury Ave.
Kew Gardens
Surrey TW9 4JF England
Phone: 44 (0) 20 8392-8585; Fax: 44 (0) 20 8392-9876
E-mail: info@bushwoodbooks.co.uk
Website: www.bushwoodbooks.co.uk
Free postage in the U.K., Europe; air mail at cost.

Contents

Acknowledgments...4

Preface 5

Introduction: **Shoe Culture** 7

1. **The Decorative, Delicate Foot**: 1790-1900 19

2. **The Elegant Ankle**: 1900-1920 36

3. **Galoshes and Charleston Shoes**: 1920-1930 44

4. **The Swagger Years**: 1930-1940 52

5. **Platforms and Yankee-Catchers**: 1940-1950................62

6. **High Fashion Heels**: 1950-1960.....................................71

7. **Youth Fashion**: 1960-1970 87

8. **Funky Excess**: 1970-1980 112

9. **New Age Romantic Meets Sneaker Chic**: 1980-1990... 117

10. **Designer Must-Haves**: 1990-2000............................121

11. **Shoes On Fire**: 2000 127

12. **Designer Profile**: Danny Sullivan 143

Conclusion: **These Boots Were Made Fo**r Walking 148

Glossary: **Talking the Walk** 149

Bibliography..158

Index 160

Acknowledgements

Clark Bernat, managing director of the *Niagara Historical Society Museum*, unwraps a carefully preserved shoe.

My thanks to the following persons and organizations for their assistance with this book: Ellen Adamsons, Peter Banting, Clark Bernat, Helen Booth, Patricia Boyle, *Brightfeet®*, Jerilyn Brown, Marilyn Bumstead, *Capri Shoes*, Brian Carrillo, Christa Ciccolini, Kathy Crow, Kathryn Crowder, Heather Darch, Janet Dear, Tarsicio De La Torre, Lucy Evans, Susan Famolare, John Fluevog, Stephen Fluevog, *Fluevog Shoes*, Bruce Gray, Roslyn Herman, Marion Hunter, *Irregular Choice Shoes*, *Jordan Museum*, Howard Kerbel, Josh Kerbel, Erica Kubersky, the *Lake-of-the-Woods Museum*, Gale McQueen, Marie Minaker, Ron Minaker, *Minden Hills Museum*, *Musée Missisquoi*, *MooShoes,* Danielle Nason, *Niagara Historical Society & Museum*, Kyle Pickering, Suzanne Quéry, John Ruffo, Laura Russell, Marilyn Sararus, *Scentco,* John Shandor, Ardra Shephard, Corinne Shephard, Jim Shephard, Carol Simmons, Mariana Singer, David Standish, *Star Wares Collectibles*, Maia Sulkowski, Danny Sullivan, Jack Townsend, Marcia Tysseling, Kevin Vick, Avery Wham, Rachel White, and especially the *Schiffer Publishing* team.

Preface

All God's chillun got shoes. - From *Topper Takes a Trip* by Thorne Smith

If hats were my first love as a child, then shoes were my second obsession. My mother's cousin, Gene Champagne, used to relate how as a toddler, I would untie my booties, toddle over to him with my white leather treasures in hand, and demand, "whoos, whoos"; whereupon, he would pick me up, place the shoes on my feet, and wait for me to repeat the performance. I am told that the procedure went on endlessly.

As I got older, I stepped into my mother's shoes at every opportunity. Sliding my little feet into the sharply pointed toes of her stilettos (I was a child in the 50s), I was able to shuffle along, but not feel that I was really wearing them. So...I spent my preschool years in plastic Cinderella slippers. I had dozens of pairs of these pretend high heels in various colours. The sparkly temptations, which were affixed to cardboard inside a cello bag, hung at kids-eye level at our local five-and-dime. A band of coloured elastic stretched across the bridge of each foot to keep the shoes in place and add to their allure.

At the age of five, I was introduced to soft leathery ballet slippers. I loved their feel, their smell, and their promise of glittery costumes and recitals. I continued in dance until the age of sixteen, but escaped the torture of ballet pointes.

I wore sturdy shoes at school and jumped rope in them at recess until I wore holes in the soles. On wet days I skipped through puddles in shiny yellow rubbers. My mother laments that I was "very hard" on my shoes and required numerous replacements that had nothing to do with growth or size changes.

Annual back-to-school shopping trips included a fitting at *Tot and Teen Footwear* when we lived in Hamilton. It was here that I saw

The author's favourite shoes - a pair of kitty-themed walkabouts. Label: *Anarchic™ 2002*.

Detail.

into the structure of my feet by standing on an x-ray device. This allowed the salesman and my mother to determine whether or not my new saddle shoes compressed the bones of my feet. My friend Debby, who accompanied us on these excursions, always hated her new school shoes and would attempt to scuff them up before leaving the store, a dreadful sin in my estimation.

Debby and I had differing opinions on sneakers as well. When we raced, the winner always credited the success to her superior footwear, which, at the time, were flat canvas runners that had yet to sprout heels.

My winter boots were fur-lined and cozy until I reached my teens; it was then that I endured frostbite in my for-looks-only, knee-high zippered vamps. By then, go-go boots were the rage, but I preferred flat sandals with self-fabric laces that wrapped around my calves. I think that is how I snagged my husband.

I tried working at a shoe store as a student, but was turned down for the sales position. Perhaps I exhibited too much enthusiasm. I am capable of whipping it up even over men's shoes. One of the guests at my wedding positively dazzled in a pair of 70's stars-and-stripes oxfords. I made certain his feet were in the wedding photographs.

Married life in rural Quebec brought the unique adventure of shopping for discount shoes in an old barn. The proprietor of this five-dollar-a-pair emporium was as keen to sell as I was to buy; so much so, that one night we braved a thunderstorm in order to make our transaction. By the yellow glare of a kerosene lamp I sorted through a mountain of boxes to purchase seven pairs of disco heels.

I hated my nursing shoes – "duty shoes" they were called. These required endless polishing and disinfecting; and worse, they made my ankles look thick. I received many a dressing down for my nonconformity in this area. I had been hospitalized in France, and remembered that my Parisian nurses wore any frivolous little shoe that took their fancy. These looked so good with their jewellery and lifted the spirits of their patients. Ah well.

On the day of my daughter's wedding I discovered the horror of doggy-tooth marks in the navy linen strappies, around which, I had built my mother-of-the-bride ensemble. Unwilling to give them up, I made the damaged goods precious by adding millinery orchids to the toes and heels. I enjoyed whispered remarks about them as I walked down the aisle. A shoemaker later told me that he owes much of his business to the society of dogs.

Today my feet long for designer heels and vintage, jewelled *Roger Viviers*; but with grandchildren on the horizon, I find myself gravitating to little leather booties. "Whoos". Hmmm. Perhaps my love affair with shoes is beginning all over again.

The same hot shoe - this time in lipstick-red patent leather. *Private Collection*. $60 when new.

Back patent leather ankle straps on a ½-inch gold platform. Matching 3½-inch gold heels. Label: *Michael Antonia. Private Collection*. $60 when new.

Introduction
Shoe Culture

Shoes require special attention because they are an accessory that completes an outfit. - Desginer Georgio Armani

Great shoes transcend eras. - Deborah Fulsang, fashion reporter

My shoes and messages are quite simply, part of me. - John Fluevog, shoe designer.

(Fluevog is known for his avant-garde designs and offbeat humor. His shoes have been worn by Madonna, James Spader, and Robin Williams and immortalized on fun and funky stamps by Canada Post.)

Shoes: the scent of leather, the click of a stiletto on hardwood, the slippery coolth of a satin bedroom slipper; no other item of apparel is so closely related to the senses. At times shoes have even stood in for champagne vessels. And while the *Fluevog* company, with their jellybean "shoe polish", invites customers to "taste our mouth-watering shoes" pastry chefs are taking the shoe/taste connection a step further, creating cakes and cookies in popular footwear designs.

I see beauty in every sole: These frosted plastic shoeboxes by *ShoeStor* enable a shoe lover to see her complete collection at a glance.

Fluevog Shoe Store, Toronto, ON.

John Fluevog's *Audry*: A wineglass heel acts as a pedestal for a red crackle pump with black stitching. *Courtesy of Stephen Fluevog*. $155 new.

John Fluevog's blue toe sandal. *Courtesy of Stephen Fluevog*.

John Fluevog's *Cecily*: Black with pink, bow-trimmed pump. *Courtesy of Stephen Fluevog*. $199 new.

John Fluevog's *Miss June*: This striking peep-toe wraps the foot in a soft and subtle bow. *Courtesy of Stephen Fluevog.*

John Fluevog's *Pink Nun*: This twin-strap walking shoe prominently displays a Fluevog logo. *Courtesy of Stephen Fluevog.*

John Fluevog's *Jolene*: This femme version of the rebel boot with its multiple bindings, hints at bondage. *Courtesy of Stephen Fluevog.*

John Fluevog's *Selina*: The Fluevog logo can be clearly seen on the insole of this pretty blue slide. *Courtesy of Stephen Fluevog.*

Shoe designer, John Fluevog. *Courtesy of Stephen Fluevog.*

9

Who Collects Shoes?

Imelda Marcos, the former Philippine First Lady and the world's most infamous shoe collector, was reported to have owned 3,000 pair of shoes during her husband's presidency. Her stash quickly became a symbol of extravagance when opposition forces toppled the Marcos government in 1986. Much of the collection, including the espadrilles she wore when fleeing the presidential palace, is now on exhibit to the public at the footwear museum in the Philippine city of Marikina. "Filipinos recycle the bad into things of beauty," said Marcos, at the opening of the facility.

Many shoe lovers own more pairs than they can reasonably wear in one year. Actress and self-proclaimed shoe lover, Constance Marie, admitted to owning one hundred and fifteen pair, when she appeared on the *Martha Stewart Show* in February 2006. She purchased three additional pairs while in New York for the taping.

Law librarian, Betty Dykstra, collects new and wearable vintage shoes. The self-confessed "shoe-aholic" ("I can't start buying because I can't stop"), keeps sandpaper in her desk for scuffing up the soles of new shoes, on those occasions when freshly polished floors are particularly slick.

Some shoe hoarders report an emotional attachment to their favourite shoes, and are able to recite their history; when and where they were purchased, on what occasion they were worn, or what was happening in their life at the time. Indeed, the shoe sagas are closely related to their personal memoirs; similarly, vintage fashion enthusiasts purchase period footwear in order to connect with a favored historical era.

Ultra-expensive footwear is often purchased for a different reason, however. Michael Fink, the senior director of fashion at *Saks Fifth Avenue*, believes that many high-priced shoes currently on the retail market are purchased by collectors as art objects. They "go directly into a display case and never see a foot," believes Fink.

True shoe aficionados enjoy wearing, shopping for, or simply looking at, their shoes. Author and designer, Christy Ferer, incorporated a famous shoe image into her home décor, by superimposing a photo of the Duchess of Windsor's shoe closet onto a muslin room divider. Seven rows of soft-hued pumps and ankle straps face forward, creating an aura of simple elegance.

The mere sight of that perfect pair of shoes will cause a serious shoe hound to bite or even lick her lips; likewise, a rare antique find might send the most staid museum curator into a swoon. One visitor to Montreal's *McCord Museum* told me she was transfixed by a particularly exquisite display of children's shoes; so much so, that she had to remind herself to breathe. Is it any wonder; then, that shoe lovers form collectors clubs, produce shoe videos, organize sneaker subculture events, and subscribe to magazines dedicated solely to shoe collecting?

Shoes have even caught the attention of art thieves in recent years; notably, the ruby slippers heist, which occurred at the *Judy Garland Museum* in August 2005, and the taking of a $160,000 pair of rare, jewel-encrusted, princely shoes, from the *Bata Shoe Museum* in January 2006.

Images of shoes on television and in the print media possess the power to shape a culture and influence commerce. In the 1950s, the innovative, blotted-ink and rubberstamp images of shoes by commercial and pop artist, Andy Worhol, sparked the imagination of buyers, and helped to revitalize the *I. Miller Shoe Company* of New York. Half a century later, the shoe-buying habits of television characters like *Sex in the City*'s Carrie Bradshaw catapulted such notable footwear designers as Manolo Blahnik and Jimmy Choo to the pinnacle of success.

In January, 2006, *Forbes Magazine* reported the world's most costly retail shoes to be a pair of Manolo Blahnik alligator boots, offered for sale at $14,000 (US). The purchase of ultra-expensive footwear escalated in the latter half of 2005, due in part to designer footwear being profiled in pop culture. The design, workmanship, fine materials, costly and often rare embellishments that are involved in the creation of such items, also serve to increase their value.

Shoes bear witness to our existence; our adventures, our stamina, the very paths we have trod. They are sculptural testaments to our lives and times; in truth, tangible evidence of our having walked the earth. The shoes within these pages have taken first steps, gone to school, danced at weddings, even stood in bread lines. They have seen loved ones off to war, teetered at cocktail parties, attended freedom demonstrations, rock concerts, and more.

Toronto's *Bata Shoe Museum* where a pair of rare jewel-encrusted slippers were stolen and recovered, following an anonymous phone call.

Queen of Collectibles

The surface of the shoes seemed to pulse with hundreds of reflections and refractions. In the firelight it was like looking at boiling corpuscles of blood under a magnifying glass. - From *Wicked* by Gregory Maguire

Commercially, Dorothy's ruby slippers worn by Judy Garland in the 1939 film classic *The Wizard of Oz*, are the queen of collectibles. One pair fetched $600,000.00 US when auctioned at *Christies* in May of 2000. Several pairs exist, including one on permanent exhibit at the *Smithsonian Institute*, and another owned by Hollywood memorabilia collector, Michael Shaw. This pair was reported stolen August 28, 2005 from the *Judy Garland Museum* in Grand Rapids, Minnesota, where the famous shoes were on loan for the ten-week summer season.

The red-sequined movie version shoes differ in appearance from the silver slippers originally scripted in L. Frank Baum's early twentieth-century fairy tale, as screen tests at *MGM* found the color to be unsuitable for film. *MGM* screenwriter Noel Langley made the noteworthy change. Whether they be red or silver; however, there is no denying the captivating nature of the coveted slippers.

Gregory Maguire developed the concept of the enchanted shoes further in his novel *Wicked; The Life and Times of the Wicked Witch of the West.* Within his book, the ruby slippers captivate various characters for diverse reasons, yet Glinda, the good witch who has resoled the pretty slippers and imbued them with power through a magic spell, fully recognizes their basic mundane nature. She tells Elphaba that the Munchkinlanders "put too much credit in those silly shoes. I mean, a magic sword I could understand, but shoes? Please."

The shoes or their replicas, with their suggestion of residual magic, cropped up at so many public ceremonies that, like the relics of saints, they began to multiply to fill the need. - From *Wicked* by Gregory Maguire

Oz fan, Jack Townsend has been creating replica ruby slippers for the past twenty years. Although he hasn't kept a record of how many pairs he has sold, Townsend estimates that he responds to about seventy ruby-slipper enquiries annually. His creations purport to be accurate facsimiles of the famous footwear, down to the orange felt that lined the bottom of Dorothy's shoes in the yellow brick road scene. Townsend's shoes with their re-created *Innes* label, have been exhibited at the *Yellow Brick Road Museum*, Indiana, the *MGM Grand Hotel* in Las Vegas, and the *Judy Garland Museum* in Minnesota.

Q & A: Jack Townsend

What is it about Dorothy's ruby slippers that makes them so sought after?

To some people they represent hope. Oz fans think of them as a talisman; an object possessing the magical ability to take them home, or return them to a place where they can be happy once again.

How did you get started creating the replica ruby slippers?

I saw the originals at the *Smithsonian*, and I wanted a pair for myself. Through the years I researched pictures and diagrams until I was able to craft an exact facsimile.

Who buys your shoes?

Collectors, Halloween costumers, actresses, Oz fans, and brides.

Brides?

Yes, brides will order them in their own shoe size to wear down the aisle. Some ask me to send them the plain shoes first to see if they fit. Then they send them back to be finished.

What is involved in creating the ruby slippers?

There about twenty steps in the process. It takes me anywhere from two to eight weeks to complete a pair. I can only work for three hours at a time. After that my hand might cramp.

Shoes as Indicators of Status

There is really nothing in the world that can be compared to red shoes! - From *The Red Shoes* by Hans Christian Andersen

Unique footwear or embellishments may reflect personal expression and individuality, or one's station within a particular religious, imperial, or other organizational hierarchy. Shoes are a foundational element of ceremonial dress, serving visually to set the wearer apart from common society through color, quality, design, workmanship, decoration, and cost. Consider the media attention garnered by Pope Benedict XVI's red Prada loafers, or Queen Elizabeth II's garnet-studded, gold kid coronation shoes designed by Roger Vivier.

At times shoes were so costly that individuals took care to list them within the contents of their estates, bequeathing them to future generations. Is it any wonder that Beau Brummell, the father of dandyism, recommended polishing one's boots with champagne?

A great deal of information about shoes has been gleaned through the preservation of estate and other historical documents, but footwear knowledge and related artefacts have also survived due to superstitious beliefs. Shoes found in demolitions and archaeological digs; for example, may have been carefully hidden in dwellings centuries ago, in the belief that they possessed the ability to ward off evil spirits. And the following "shoeperstitions" persist to this day:

- Walking with one shoe on and one shoe off is believed by some to bring bad luck for an entire year.
- Some believe that shoes placed on a table or chair, on the bed, under the bed, or above one's head will attract misfortune.
- Shoes tied together and hung from a nail are considered by some to be a precursor to calamity.
- Some believe that shoes left in the shape of a cross must be picked up by another person; in order to reverse bad luck.
- Placing one's left foot on the ground first in the morning, is thought by some to ensure a "bad day".

Others believe the following practices will ensure good fortune:

- Wearing old shoes on Friday the 13th.
- Always using the right foot when crossing a threshold.
- Placing an old shoe outside the front door before setting out on a journey.
- Filling one's shoes with ferns to attract prosperity.
- Throwing shoes at a newly wedded couple, or tying shoes to the bumper of their car, is thought to ensure a happy marriage.

Many a matador has also been pelted with the shoes of eligible women following a successful bullfight.

1847: *Punch Magazine's* satirical look at how one's footwear might express one's political affiliation.

PRINCE ALBERT "AT HOME."
WHEN HE WILL SUSTAIN NO END OF DIFFERENT CHARACTERS.

1847: An illustration of various "characters" each with distinct footwear.

PARTY BOOTS.

IT is an old saying, "Tell me what company you keep, and I will tell you what you are;" but we say, "If you want a character, let us look at your boots, and we will give you one." Phrenologists may fumble over the head; but looking at the heads of politicians to form an estimate of the quality, we soon discover that there is nothing in them—the sole is the true criterion for judging of a man's pos-ition, dis-position, or even his in-dis-position to serve the interests of his fellow-creatures. Let us make a brief examination of a few pairs of boots and shoes, that we may judge of the standing their wearers are entitled to.

As Whiggery happens to have a pretty firm footing just now, let us examine the *chaussure* of that party. Here we find the understanding in tolerably good order, but there is an exhibition of foppery which is not quite agreeable, and which would prevent the owner from taking the straightforward path if there seemed to be anything in the way that might prove a little inconvenient. The Whig *chaussure* does not seem quite so well adapted as it ought to be for going boldly on wherever duty directs, regardless of an occasional mess into which all are liable to fall, but which any one with a stout sole and a good serviceable understanding may easily go through, with a fair amount of perseverance and courage. LORD MORPETH's retiring over-delicacy with regard to the Health of Towns Bill shows the peculiarity of the Whig *chaussure*, which partakes a great deal more of the weak insignificant pump than the bold boot that boots not where it goes, so that the path leads in the right direction.

The Country party foot-gear is of a different stamp, but is not less expressive of the position of its wearers. There is a desire to retain the top, although the thing has gone by long ago, and the pretensions to such a distinction have become utterly ridiculous.

The Young England, or DISRAELI *chaussure*, is something really melancholy to contemplate. There is a sad indication of being on its last legs, and the curl of the toe bespeaks that all is up with this unhappy section of politicians. Even Holywell Street, with all its associations, would refrain from naming a price for this worn-out remnant of "leather and prunella."

High Church and Low Church are strongly marked in the article which now occupies our attention. The boots of the former evince a starched stiffness truly characteristic of the spirit that animates their wearer; but it is "quite another pair of shoes" with Low Church, whose comfortable modesty bespeaks a mixture of humility and selfishness that will be found blended in a very great degree in the class we have laid by the heels in the annexed illustration. We shall wind up our gallery with the working man's *chaussure*; and any one who looks upon the picture may judge that the labourer is reduced sometimes to very shocking extremities.

13

Shoes in Art, Literature, and Pop Culture

Your shoes are your shoes. There's nothing spiritual about them. - Dick Dewert, Miracle Channel television host

In the cold and the darkness, a poor little girl, with bare head and naked feet, roamed through the streets. It is true she had on a pair of slippers when she left home, but they were not of much use. They were very large, so large, indeed, that they had belonged to her mother, and the poor little creature had lost them in running across the street to avoid two carriages that were rolling along at a terrible rate. One of the slippers she could not find, and a boy seized upon the other and ran away with it, saying that he could use it as a cradle, when he had children of his own. So the little girl went on with her little naked feet, which were quite red and blue with the cold. - From *The Red Shoes* by Hans Christian Andersen

When they appear in fairy tales, nursery rhymes, and fables, shoes often possess talismanic or magical qualities. In whatever form it takes a shoe plainly stands between ourselves - our vulnerability, even our Achilles heel - and the cold, harsh world. A shoe is literally positioned "where the rubber meets the road."

Bare feet are fine for languishing in earthy soil, sandy shores, or fields of clover; but, when stepping out of our homes, propelling ourselves forward, moving into the world about us, shoes are required. The leather-soled stockings worn by the English nobility in the middle ages; for example, would not be practical for anyone outside of the leisure classes. Similarly, no arduous labour can be performed in high heels.

There was an old woman who lived in a shoe. - From the *Mother Goose* nursery rhyme

Ann Thomas, in her book *The Women We Become,* views shoes with their intimate contact with the ground or mother earth, as symbolic of the feminine aspect of personality. Thomas reports, "Shoes have qualities of nurturing – keeping us warm, dry, protected from cuts and bruises – and other qualities of holding and containing, that are all mother attributes."

While shoes are often conspicuous by their absence in prehistoric and primitive art, footwear does appear at times on otherwise scantily-clad early Greek statuary; such as, *The Apollo Belvedere.* As well, Roman art of the 3rd to 5th century often illustrates period footwear. *The Archangel Michael;* for instance, is depicted in meticulously detailed ivory sandals.

Commissioned and self-portraits, such as that of Peter Paul Rubens' *Self-Portrait with Isabella Brant* and Anthony van Dyck's *Portrait of Charles I Hunting,* provide accurate renderings of the footwear of their day. Costume depictions in fine art outside of this genre; however, can make strong political and/or moral statements, as in Master Bertram's *Cain Slaying Abel* in which the eye is drawn to the strongly patterned poulaines worn by the murderous brother. This painting is as much a reflection of the church's view on the popular shoe style, as it is a depiction of the famous story.

Now we are boys so fine to see, Why should we longer cobblers be? - From the children's fable *The Elves and the Shoemaker*

The citation or illustration of shoes in art and literature serves a dual function; educating historians on the development of footwear in the absence of extant examples, and giving substance to intangible concepts through the practice of allegory. Whereas portraiture is of particular value in the first instance; still-lifes or *nature-mortes* such as Van Gogh's paintings of shoes in 1886 and 1887, tend to serve the latter purpose.

At times, certain written references to shoes achieve both objectives; as in the following line from the second act of *Hamlet, Prince of Denmark,* "By'r lady, your ladyship is nearer heaven than when I saw you last, by the altitude of a chopine." Thanks to the bard modern-day researchers are able to assign a knowledge of the chopine to seventeenth-century England, but to an audience of Shakespeare's contemporaries, this utterance would have had deeper, if not comic, interpretation, given the Church's stand (pun intended) on this controversial style.

Children acquire an early understanding of the importance of shoes through fables, fairy tales, myths, and legends. Young minds take delight in the concept of charmed footwear, and learn cultural expectations of behaviour along the way. "There was once a girl who trod on a loaf to avoid soiling her shoes, and the misfortunes that happened to her in consequence are well known." So begins Aesop's fable *The Girl Who Trod On The Loaf.* The girl is described as proud and presuming, and the fable makes the distinction between the virtue of purity and the sin of conceit, through the symbolism of the shoes. "So Inge put on her new shoes...and set out, stepping very carefully, that she might be clean and neat about the feet, and there was nothing wrong in doing so." Inge's misdeed occurs rather, when she sacrifices a loaf of bread intended for her impoverished mother, in order to protect her pretty shoes; consequently, she sinks into a marsh and disappears into a place of suffering and torment.

In the *Galoshes of Fortune,* Aesop again uses footwear to expose human nature. This time a pair of magic boots is empowered to instantly transport the unsuspecting wearer to a time and place of his desire. The messenger of fortune and the fairy of care argue over whether the galoshes will bring happiness or unhappiness to mankind.

Every woman dreams of being Cinderella, and Cinderella's fantasy shoe has finally become a reality. - Stuart Weitzman, celebrity shoe designer

Cinderella's famous glass slippers present us with another example of fabled footwear. Although the shoes (made of *vair* or squirrel fur in the early French version) have morphed (through improper translation) into the more familiar glass (*verre*) slippers, they remain emblematic of transformation in a classic story that illuminates the interplay between spirit and matter.

The fantasy shoes continue to motivate today as evidenced by the pair recreated in diamonds by fantasy-shoe guru, Stuart Weitzman, for the 2005 Academy Awards. Weitzman holds the record for designing the most expensive shoes ever; Oz-inspired ruby slippers, woven from platinum thread, and set with 642 rubies.

A shoe tree.

Vintage *Stuart Weitzman* label.

Character Shoes/Theatrical Footwear

In a Gershwin show I wore some brutal, show-girl, shoes - silver high heels. I don't remember much about them except that they were painful, because they belonged to the wardrobe department. - Ardra Shephard, singer/actress

Many shoe collectors form sub-specialty collections of theatrical footwear, or focus exclusively on "show shoes", which may be desirable due to their workmanship, or because of a celebrity or fantasy association.

The responsibility of a costumer regarding shoes is in ordering, buying, painting, or adapting shoes to a particular role. Theatrical shoes can be modified through the addition of taps or other devices to create a particular sound. A character may require a shuffling walk; for example, or a school principal may need to click threateningly down the hall. A heavy shoe; for instance, might be a reflection of the "weight" of the character.

In addition to conferring status or representing task or personality traits, character shoes must at times, replicate an era. Special skill is required in creating such footwear fitted to modern feet. When actors are required to carry out exceptional manoeuvres; such as, back flips or jumps, additional factors need to be considered. Hinges or metal braces might be placed between the heel and the sole of their shoes, for support and ease of movement.

Often theatrical shoes need to appear fragile or delicate, yet be safe and sturdy. Some performers may be called upon to glide across the stage on wheels, or do acrobatics. Costumers must deal with the unexpected as well. During a *Confederation Place* performance of

Canada Rocks; for example, the shoes of a singer had to be changed when the heels of her fragile mules kept getting caught in the space between the stage and the orchestra pit. Given the importance of footwear to an actor's stage presence and performance, it comes as no surprise that there are even more footwear superstitions in the theatre than among the general population; indeed, the sound of squeaking shoes upon an actor's initial stage entrance is thought to be a good omen.

The movies have their own footwear history; although, shoes played only a minor role in cinema until the glamour years of the thirties. Before talking pictures, film stars wore their own shoes on set, but during the thirties the reverse was true. Movie stars often borrowed eveningwear from the studios to wear to Hollywood social functions, where they expected to be photographed.

Brown and gold men's character shoes, worn by Vincent Price for his role as Baka in *The Ten Commandments.* Laces (not shown) are of gold metallic rope. Shoes bear an enamelled lotus insignia. *Courtesy of Star Wares Collectibles & Larry's Shoe Museum.* Value undisclosed.

Today television and film industry costumers are challenged by animal-rights actors who insist that no animals be harmed in the making of their costumes. Synthetic clogs were fashioned for Joachin Pheonix; for example, when he performed in *Quills,* and non-leather cowboy boots were ordered for his portrayal of Johnny Cash in *Walk the Line.* Fashionable non-leather shoes have become increasingly available through companies like *MooShoes Inc.,* a New York retailer that sells "cruelty-free" footwear and accessories.

Shoes worn on and off set by Hollywood screen idols are readily available to collectors today, through websites and dealers of studio clothes and movie memorabilia. One such outlet; *Roslyn Herman & Co.,* who have been selling authentic celebrity apparel

for twenty-five years, offer certificates of authenticity with their merchandise. Herman acquired many of her vintage artefacts from consignee, Gordon Bau (*Warner Brothers* one time make-up chief). "Hollywood stars of the 20s, 30s and 40s would often gift Bau with personal possessions in lieu of cash, when he worked for them privately," remembers Herman.

Alicia Red Espadrilles by *MooShoes. Courtesy of Avery Wham.* $65 new.

MooShoes' Coyote: These fringed boots are crafted entirely of manmade materials. *Courtesy of Avery Wham.* $59.95 new.

MooShoes' Lulu (brown): Flat boots with beaded tassels. Manmade materials. *Courtesy of Avery Wham.* $85 new.

Mooshoes' Mary sandal of manmade materials. *Courtesy of Avery Wham*. $45.95 new.

The same boot in black. This view shows the top-stitched vamp and centre seam. *Courtesy of Avery Wham.* $85 new.

Mooshoes' Samurai boot of manmade materials. *Courtesy of Avery Wham*.

These dressy, *MooShoes* thongs are crafted entirely of manmade materials. *Courtesy of Avery Wham*.

The Social Significance of Shoes

Most women, I think, could look back and tell their own stories through their shoes. The shoes you fell in love with at different stages of your life say a lot about who you were then. - Jane Eldershaw, *Heart and Sole, the Shoes of My Life*

The first pair of shoes that I recall wearing were wooden ones. They had rough leather on the top, but the bottoms, which were about an inch thick, were of wood. When I walked they made a fearful noise, and besides this they were very inconvenient since there was no yielding to the natural pressure of the foot. - Booker T. Washington, 19th -century slave

Women express themselves through their shoes. - Christian Louboutin, shoe designer

Notwithstanding the practical purpose of shoes — safety, defence against the elements, support for the foot — this costume item has served throughout history as a powerful indicator of class, gender identity, profession, military rank, affluence, position, or lack thereof. Eighteenth-century slaves in the Carolinas; for example, generally went barefoot. In fact, Grand Juries complained when legislation for preventing the "excessive and costly apparel of Negroes and other slaves" failed to be enacted. Boston King, in his memoirs of growing up in slavery in Charlestown, South Carolina, wrote, "Being obliged to travel in different parts of America with racehorses, I suffered many hardships. Happening one time to lose a boot belonging to the groom, he would not suffer me to have any shoes all that winter, which was a great punishment to me."

Reports of slave runaways took careful note of their footwear. A woman named Molly, who had four restraint devices attached to her legs, managed to escape in high-heeled shoes; while another named Road, broke out in a pair of "leather shoes with wooden heels." Historian Philip Morgan uncovered the remarkable story of Will, a rural slave who, denied access to the fashionable footwear of the day, went so far as to have the skin of his legs gouged "in the exact form of ribbed stockings." Perhaps these individuals were aware of the ability of footwear to communicate unspoken information about the wearer, and thereby affect the attitude of the beholder.

The poor boy changes clothes
And puts on after-shave
To compensate for his ordinary shoes - Paul Simon, singer/songwriter

Today shoes continue to serve as cultural indicators. Stephen Hull, in his sociological study of the surfing subculture, identifies "slaps, thongs, and tennis shoes" as part of the uniform of the Santa Cruz surfer; likewise, police and sheriff's departments include athletic shoe brand names when compiling lists of possible gang-member identifiers. And while street gangs configure and color-coordinate shoe lacings, Argentine artist Judy Werthein dangles flashlights and compasses from the red, white, and green *Brinco*® sneakers she distributes to Mexican migrants.

Chapter One

The Decorative, Delicate Foot: 1790-1900

No two women spend money on clothes in the same manner. ... those with pretty feet will want more for hosen and shoen, those who look best in hats will claim the lion's share for millinery. - From *The Dress Allowance, What's What, 1902*

The high-heeled shoes associated with the aristocracy were abandoned following the French revolution, in favour of flat, leather slippers, which reflected the politically correct notion of equality. The plain, low-walled shoes contrasted sharply with the heavily embellished, silk footwear worn by the upper classes prior to 1790. These longwearing shoes that could be easily repaired, remained in style (with variations in toe shape) until the advent of the hoop skirt at mid-century.

The advancement c.1830, of the galoshed leather boot, allowed women greater freedom of movement outdoors, although fabric slippers remained popular for evening. By mid-century, mechanization enabled mass production of footwear increasing the availability of inexpensive shoes for the masses; as previously, they had been painstakingly produced by hand.

As dress styles changed, so did ladies' boots. With skirts swinging freely over wire-framed crinolines, modesty dictated that footwear rise in height to conceal the ankle; thus, the heelless, laced boot was born. The side-buttoned boot appeared c.1870, as designers chose to draw attention to the ankle; meanwhile, bustle dresses made the scene, and heels returned to complement them.

The two-inch Louis heel and shorter, "baby" Louis worked in concert with the new dress style to showcase the derrière; and as skirts fell straighter in the front, it became necessary to embellish the toe and vamp, which was now revealed. This was accomplished with beads, bows, and embroidery; indeed, *Harpers Bazaar*, c.1877, shows a black patent leather evening slipper, lined with purple silk on white faille, to match a purple satin heel. The vamp is adorned with a purple satin, fan-shaped bow, set with a silver buckle. Garlands of leaves trail from the bow along the sides of the slipper to the open heel. The popular American fashion journal advised that such footwear ought to be trimmed with bands and buttons in the color or material of one's dress.

C.1830-1840: Galoshed, blue silk Adelaides; white fabric lining, size 5. These shoes were made by A. W. Walter of Woodbury, Ct. for Helen McKean, a granddaughter of Thomas McKeon, one of the fifty-six who signed the *American Declaration of Independence. Musée Missisquoi.* A similar item might sell for $300-350.

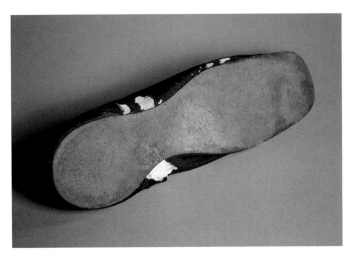

Underview showing worn leather sole.

Shoes for daywear and outdoor boots were similarly fancified with scallops, Vandyked edgings, contrasting materials, braid, and ornamental stitching; with the result that, footwear was anything but understated. Accessory-crazed Victorians went even further by applying removable frills, buckles, and immense ribbon bows to their footwear; particularly, silk ball shoes that out of vanity and class-consciousness, were worn outdoors in all weather. Ruched or pleated lace, silk-and-satin shoe rosettes took on numerous configurations. Often the entire shoe was fabricated to match a particular gown, and stockings were patterned from toe to mid-calf to complement an ensemble. Many fine examples may be found in costume museums worldwide, including a golden silk pair embroidered with roses, housed at the Union Français des Arts du Costume.

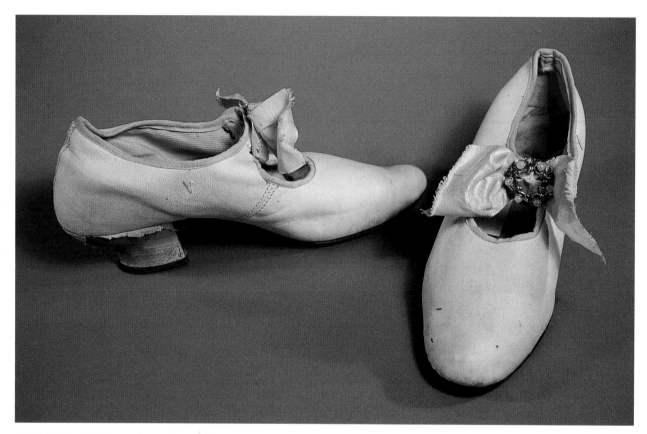

1891: White kid, bow-trimmed wedding shoes worn by bride Mrs. Marvin Smith. Inside the toe is found a tarnished silver halfpenny minted in 1823. *Musée Missisquoi.* A similar item might sell for $350-400.

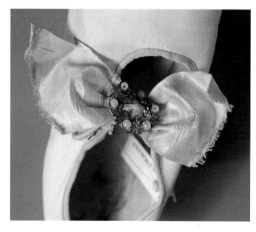

Detail: A pearl-dotted wreath cinches a silk satin bow to adorn the vamp of this wedding slipper.

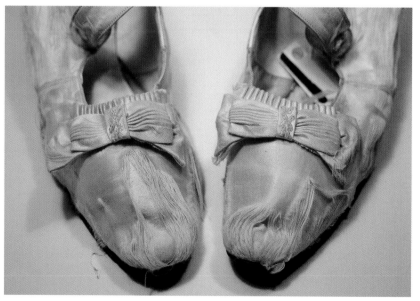

Detail: Beaded double bow adornment on a similar shoe from the same era. Arabella Fodd Bridgette wore the shoes January 13th, 1893. *Musée Missisquoi.* A similar item might sell for $300-375.

A need to accessorize white wedding gowns, which came into vogue at mid-century, resulted in the lasting tradition of white bridal slippers both in Britain and North America; conversely, black shoes stepped into the fashion arena c.1861, following the death of England's Prince Albert.

Soft, flat-heeled travelling slippers of fabric or fancy crochet-work came into vogue by the 1880s. Marketed as "Turkish" slippers, they covered the toe only or tied onto the foot with ribbon. Silk ribbon was used to lace open-fronted kid boots, and further served foot fashion by covering elastic instep bands often found on evening shoes with low-cut vamps. Low-heeled travelling shoes developed for the Victorian sport of long distance walking or pedestrianism, tied across the instep with tassel-trimmed laces; in short, austerity was reserved only for sleek, knee-high riding boots.

Plain house shoes gained approval around 1880. These low-rise slip-ons rested on ½-inch heels and were cut more for comfort than for style, with some designs offering rounded and even squared-off toes.

By the 1890s, travelling shoes rested at two to four inches above the ankle and fastened with lacing or off-center buttons. Pointed toes extended to greater and greater lengths. A decade later, Canada's *Eaton's* department store offered "something new and pretty" for fashion-conscious ladies: an ankle boot with plaid top and brown-and-black kid vamp. Teenage girls were permitted flat-soled ankle boots that buttoned along the side; one such style, offered by *Eaton's* toward the close of the century, was termed the "*Misses' boot*".

In much the same way they do today, shoemakers of the late Victorian period designed specific footwear for the various sporting pursuits in which women participated. Golf shoes, skates, and roller skates appeared alongside the gymnasium shoe - a type of ballet flat with ankle lacing. Flat shoes with knee-high spats accessorized women's hunting gear, and strappy beach shoes worn with full-length stockings, completed the bathing costume of the day. Ladies' black canvas bicycle boots, designed with narrow toes, sold for three dollars a pair in 1898, and

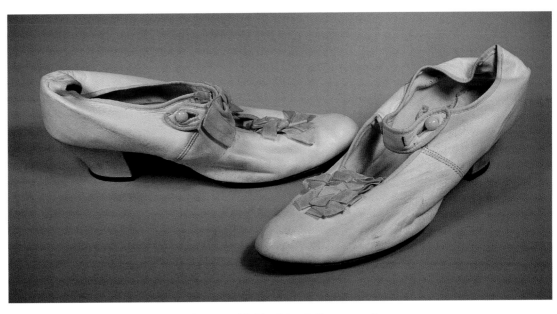

White kid, silk-trimmed wedding slippers with block heel. *Courtesy of Jordan Museum.* A similar item might sell for $275-325.

could be worn with sixty-five-cents-a-pair canvas leggings, which buttoned to the knee.

With the popularization of the bicycle came the rubber boom, and new applications for the water-proofing substance. *Goodyear*, a name associated today with tires, leant caché to shoe advertisements, which highlighted the famous name in bold print. In an age of respect for industrialization, the man who had made advancements in the process of vulcanization or the stabilization of rubber c.1839, was associated with the liberty and leisure afforded by the rubber-tired bicycle.

By the turn of the twentieth century, footwear for men and women was, for the most part, functional and colorless, yet glamorous by virtue of its fabrication and association. Men's rubber-soled shoes; for example, were marketed as bicycle boots. *Eaton's* catalogue offered a version ornamented with side "pedal patches" in chocolate and coffee-colored pebble calf.

Nineteenth century wooden clog. *Courtesy of Jordan Museum.* A similar item might sell for $200-250.

C.1850-1860: Black leather men's shoes with crossover vamp and four-button closure. Hook toe. Size 7. *Musée Missisquoi.* A similar item might sell for $325 –375.

Red leather child's boots worn by Doris Quinham of Stanbridge East. Red buttons fasten a crossover, scalloped edge closure. *Musée Missisquoi.* A similar item might sell for $80-120.

John Champion, aged three years, is shod in shiny leather shoes to complement his smart attire. *Mobile Millinery Museum and Costume Archive.*

C.1870: A child's dark brown leather shoes fasten with a buttoned ankle-strap. Brown wool pompoms adorn the toes. *Musée Missisquoi.* A similar item might sell for $80-120.

These barrette wedding shoes with Louis heel and side button closure are embellished with silver thread embroidery and glass beads. *Mobile Millinery Museum and Costume Archive.* $800-900.

Black leather Garibaldi boots with front and back grosgrain pull-tabs. Late Victorian era. Worn by Charlotte Robins. *Courtesy of Marilyn Bumstead*. A similar item might sell for $200-250.

C.1870: Brown leather, lace-up boots worn by Charlotte Robins on her wedding day. shown with the bride's gloves, purse, and floral-trimmed hat. *Courtesy of Marilyn Bumstead*. A similar item might sell for $200-250.

Detail: Shoes.

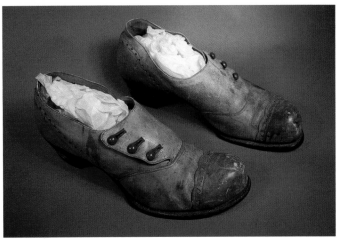

C.1850: A pair of men's caramel leather shoes with three button closure. *Courtesy of Jordan Museum*. A similar item might sell for $250-300.

1880: Black silk slippers with blue silk lining and heel strap, hand-sewn on a leather sole. Maker's mark is stamped on the sole (illegible). Size 5. *Musée Missisquoi*. A similar item might sell for $350-450.

Detail: Silk, rhinestone, and feather adornment.

Detail: The silk lining has worn away on one slipper to reveal a comfy 1-inch cushion of fleece.

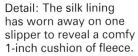

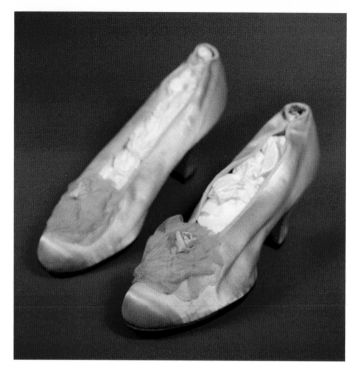

Ecru satin wedding shoes. A tulle rosette with satin centre decorates the toe. *Courtesy of Jordan Museum.* A similar item might sell for $300-350.

Early-19th-century, flat-soled slippers. *Niagara Historical Society Museum.* Value undisclosed.

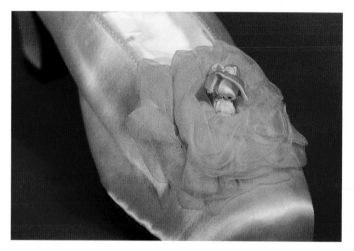

Detail: Rosette toe adornment.

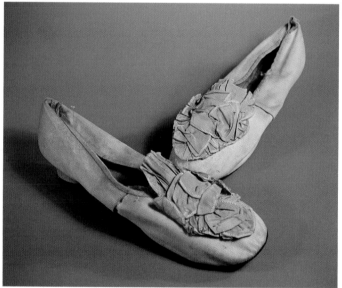

1881: Ecru satin wedding shoes made by *J. & T. Bell* of Montreal. Worn by bride Alma Daigneau Armitage of Sherbrooke, Quebec. *Musée Missisquoi.* A similar item might sell for $350-400.

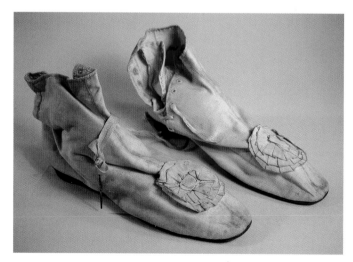

Cream canvas Adelaides with silk rosettes. *Niagara Historical Society Museum.* Value undisclosed.

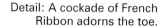

Detail: A cockade of French Ribbon adorns the toe.

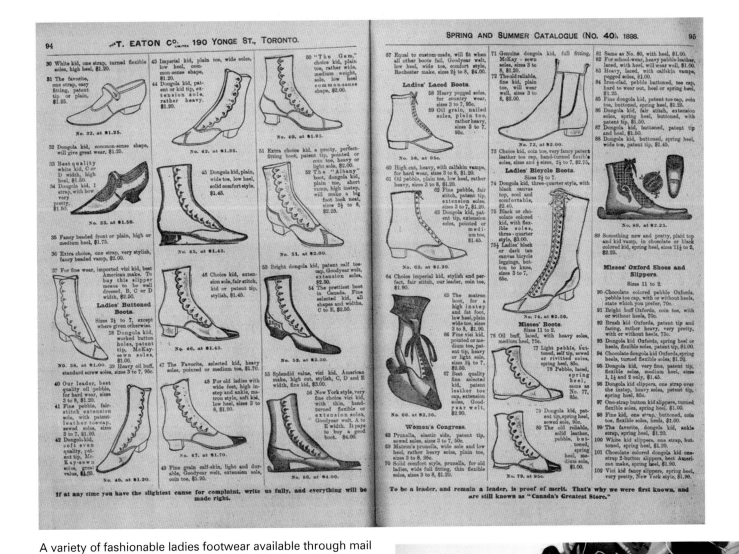

A variety of fashionable ladies footwear available through mail order, 1898. *Eaton's Spring and Summer Catalogue 1898. Courtesy of Ron Minaker.*

C.1885: Red satin Langtry with beaded vamp and toecap. Black silk laces. White fabric lining is stamped in blue with the size "3 E". Louis heel. Illegible manufacturer's mark is stamped on the leather sole. From the Sheltus family of Bedford, Quebec. *Musée Missisquoi.* A similar item might sell for $450-550.

Detail.

A trio of trading cards advertising *C. H. Ayres Shoe Store*, Bridgeport, Connecticut. *Mobile Millinery Museum and Costume Archive.* $8-12 each.

Late Victorian wool bootie with leather sole, worn by Charlotte Robins. The knitted upper was likely hand-made at home as was the custom c.1870. *Courtesy of Marilyn Bumstead.* A similar item might sell for $225-275.

Detail.

The author's great, great aunt Emily in a pair of patent tip lace ups. Late Victorian era. *Ella Philip Collection, Mobile Millinery Museum.*

The author's great aunt Margaret in a pair of laced boots. Late Victorian era. *Ella Philip Collection, Mobile Millinery Museum.*

C.1890: Ladies brown leather front lacing boots with Louis heel, toothpick toe. *Courtesy of Jordan Museum.* A similar item might sell for $250-325.

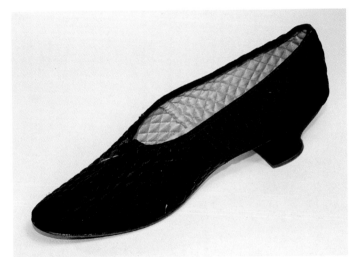

Quilted carriage slippers of black silk with pink satin lining c.1870-1890. Label: (stamped on insole) "Made in Paris for *John Barker and Co. Ltd.*, Kensington W." (by 1892 John Barker operated one of the largest and most prestigious emporiums in London, employing 1000 staff and showcasing an assortment of high-quality goods, many purchased at the *Paris Exhibitions*). *Niagara Historical Society Museum.* Value undisclosed.

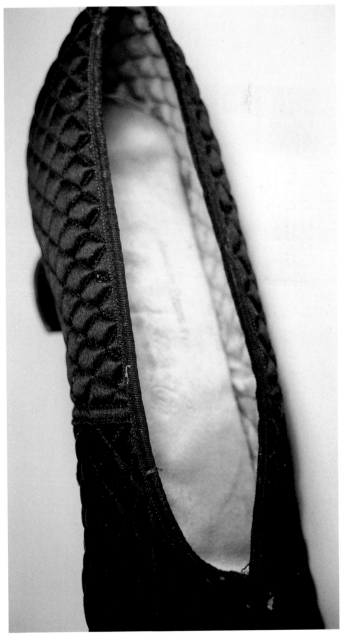

Detail.

Orange satin ball slipper c.1890, with two-inch, copper-colored heel and rhinestone toe adornment. "Jackie" is handwritten on the white leather interior of one shoe. *Niagara Historical Society Museum.* Value undisclosed.

Detail: Toe.

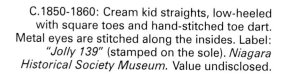

Detail: Heel.

C.1850-1860: Cream kid straights, low-heeled with square toes and hand-stitched toe dart. Metal eyes are stitched along the insides. Label: *"Jolly 139"* (stamped on the sole). *Niagara Historical Society Museum.* Value undisclosed.

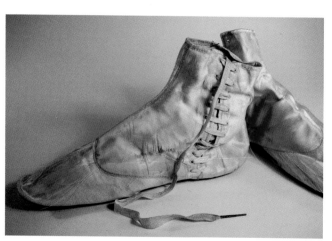

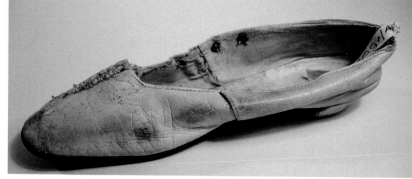

Straight-lasted, cream satin slippers with long, rounded toe. Silk lining, metal-tipped laces. Original owner: Mrs. Plumb. *Niagara Historical Society Museum.* Value undisclosed.

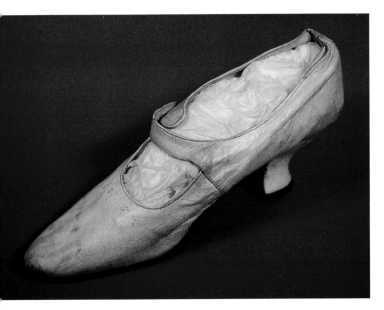

White kid slippers with block heel. *Courtesy of Jordan Museum.* A similar item might sell for $275-325.

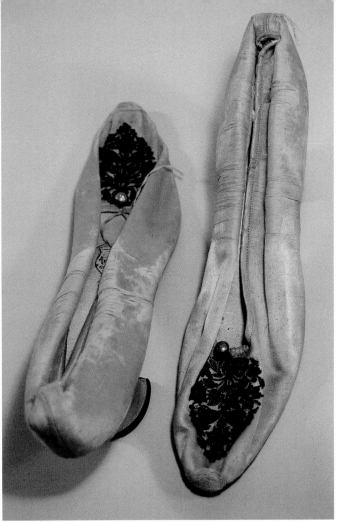

C.1870-1890: Silk slippers in pale apricot with 2-inch, Louis heels and silver bead embroidery. Drawstring closure. Label: "By Special Appointment to H.R.H. the Princess of Wales (likely Alexandra of Denmark), *Atloff & Norman*, 69 New Bond St., London. Four Prize Medals, London and Paris. "AA N" appears on the bottom of each heel. *Niagara Historical Society Museum.* Value undisclosed.

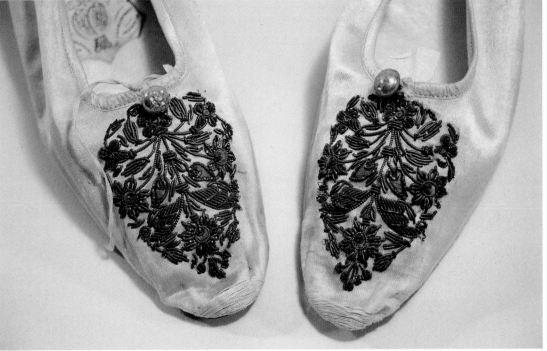

Pair of black leather high-laced shoes, made by John Kelly, of Rochester. Block heels. *Courtesy of Jordan Museum.* A similar item might sell for $250-300.

C.1870-1880: Pink satin slipper with baby Louis heel and white kid lining. Label: *Geo. T. Slater And Son"* (stamped in gold on the insole). May have been a wedding shoe as only one was preserved. *Niagara Historical Society Museum.* Value undisclosed.

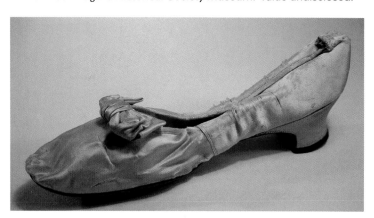

C.1870-1880: A double satin bow adorns the pointed toe of this pink silk court shoe with baby Louis heel. Possibly a wedding shoe as only one was preserved. Label: *"Atloff and Norman".* *Niagara Historical Society Museum.* Value undisclosed.

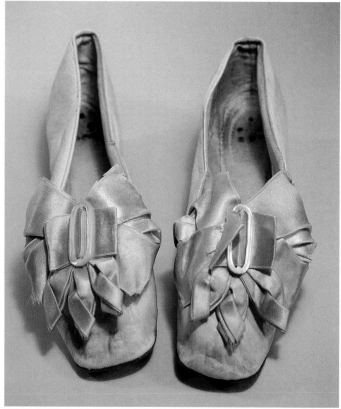

Ecru kid wedding slippers c.1870. Toes are decorated with silk Fenelon bows and white, mother-of-pearl buckles. *Niagara Historical Society Museum.* Value undisclosed.

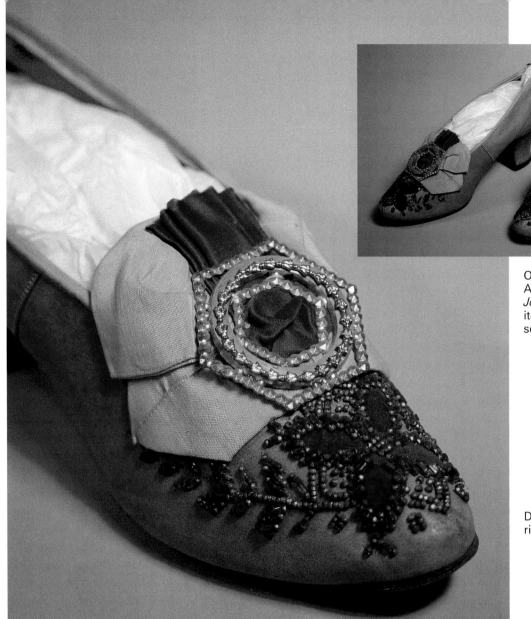

Ornate ball slippers c.1880. Apricot color. *Courtesy of Jordan Museum*. A similar item on the retail market might sell for $600-800.

Detail: Toe adorned with ribbon, buckle and beading.

Wooden-soled, beaded slides. *Niagara Historical Society Museum.* Value undisclosed.

Detail.

Detail.

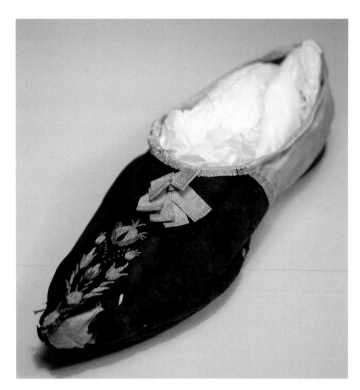

Brown and cream, straight-soled silk slippers with hand-stitched thistle motif embroidered on the toe. *Niagara Historical Society Museum.* Value undisclosed.

These knitted woollen booties have yellowed with age. One remaining pink ribbon tie. *Niagara Historical Society Museum.* Value undisclosed.

1885: Ladies ivory, high-walled satin slipper. An ivory silk cockade set with silver medallions adorns the toe. Louis heel. Label: *"Jolly 303"* imprinted on sole (*Massez Co.*). Wedding slippers of Henrietta Mcdonnell German. *Niagara Historical Society Museum.* Value undisclosed.

Detail.

Child's brown leather boots with buckle closure. Wooden soles are fitted with horseshoe-shaped metal frames at toe and heel. *Niagara Historical Society Museum.* Value undisclosed.

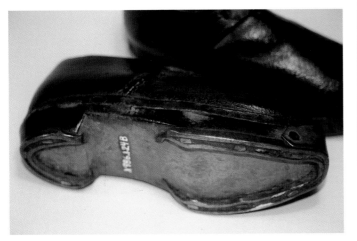

Detail.

Men's worn, shovel-toe boot with brassbound eyelets and punch-cut detail on vamp edging. "Mr. Blake" is written inside each of the shoes. Label: *Royal Quality. Rogers, Blake, and Harrisons Collection, Niagara Historical Society Museum.* Value undisclosed.

C.1855: Child's dark brown leather ankle boots with lacings and decorative black leather toe appliqué. Wooden heels. The word "Canada" is engraved on the brass toecaps. *Niagara Historical Society Museum.* Value undisclosed.

C.1850: Child's pink leather booties with scalloped edge and cream leather soles. Metal-tipped, cream-colored laces. *Niagara Historical Society Museum.* Value undisclosed.

Black leather boot with orange silk laces. *Courtesy of Jordan Museum.* A similar item might sell on the retail market for $250-350.

C.1900: Child's red leather, double eyelet boot with Van Dyked tongue and red ribbon laces. *Niagara Historical Society Museum.* Value undisclosed.

N. C. Lalonde.

PHOTO.
30 RUE ST. LAUREN

C.1890: Young Johnnie Croll in his Sunday best wears shiny patent shoes with decorative buttons. *Ella Philip Collection, Mobile Millinery Museum.*

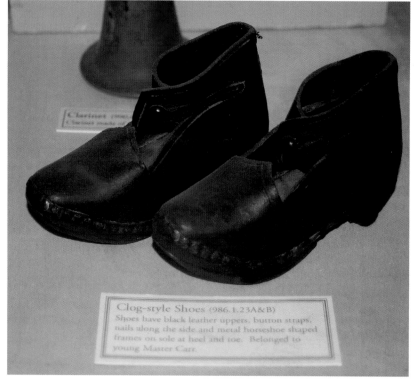

Clog-style Shoes (986.1.23A&B)
Shoes have black leather uppers, button straps, nails along the side and metal horseshoe shaped frames on sole at heel and toe. Belonged to young Master Carr.

A pair of boy's shoes on display at the *Niagara Historical Museum.* These belonged to Young Master Carr c.1850. Value undisclosed.

These lace-up boots are quite at home in their 1850s log cabin. *Courtesy of Minden Hills Museum.* A similar item might sell for $120-150.

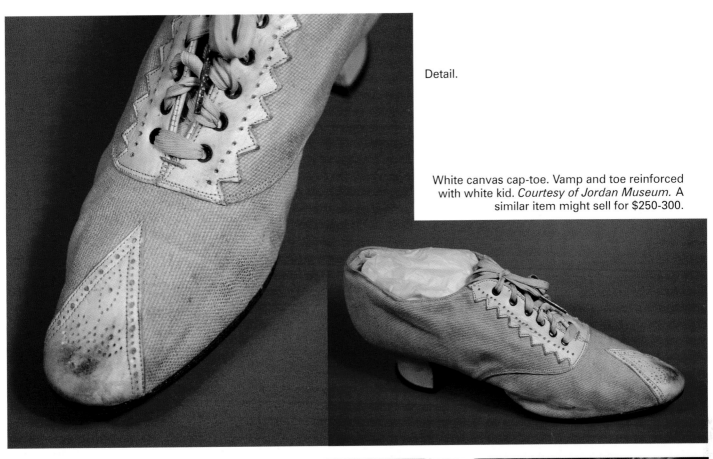

Detail.

White canvas cap-toe. Vamp and toe reinforced with white kid. *Courtesy of Jordan Museum.* A similar item might sell for $250-300.

Detail.

C.1890: Ladies toothpick-toe kid leather boots. Metal inset on French heels. *Courtesy of Jordan Museum.* A similar item might sell for $250-300.

Chapter Two

The Elegant Ankle: 1900-1920

A fat foot in a narrow tread and a long lanky foot in a short cap are equally unsuited and ridiculous. - What's What, 1902

37.

Pretty Summer Styles for Young People.

THE DELINEATOR.   DESCRIBED ON PAGE 36.   JULY, 1901.

25 B.   26 B.   27 B.   28 B.   29 B.

This sketch from the July, 1901 issue of *The Delineator* magazine illustrates in exaggerated fashion the slim-line, pointed-toe boots and children's shoes designed to set off the costumes of their day.

In a column entitled *Advice About Boots, What's What 1902* instructed that "the punishment should fit the crime." Edwardian propriety dictated that ladies with wide feet or thick ankles should avoid boots with pointy toes or slender curved heels. Those possessing dainty feet with flat insteps were encouraged to choose lace-ups with a Louis heel. The belief that feet were more attractive in close-fitting, smallish shoes caused many women to constrict their toes in tight, undersized footwear. "The uglier the foot the plainer and less obtrusive should be it's covering," proclaimed the popular London instruction manual, which further suggested that boots should be selected in accordance with one's "personal defects and qualities." Canadian advertisers were equally blunt in this regard; in fact, one department store catalogue proclaimed "EEE Width for Stout Ankles".

Vanity extended to the choice of construction materials as well as shoe style. Shiny materials, with their ability to attract the eye, were to be avoided by those individuals self-conscious about their feet. In a mail order spring-and-summer catalogue c.1900, Canada's leading department store advertised a Matron boot "for a high instep and fat foot." The low-heeled shoe with its plain wide toe, sold for $1.50. A few years later, anyone wearing these was considered out-of-date. By 1902, London style-setters declared that short-in-the-toe boots for women were so passé as to be inadmissible. The rage for pointy toes extended even to men's oxfords.

Economy-minded women; however, selected plain shoes that were not easily classed or attributed to a particular date or season. As such, their footwear outlived costlier shoes with fancy finishes, cut in accordance with a more trendy but short-lived style.

Sealskin, though expensive, produced the most durable footwear, keeping its shape for five or six years in succession. Thin, but hardwearing and almost waterproof, sealskin could be worn comfortably in both winter and summer, due to its insulating properties. Tooled Moroccan leather, ooze-calf, and ooze-sheep were next in price and comfort, although many women reserved their leather shoes for bad weather only, finding them stiff, hot, and heavy for general wear. Smooth and glacé kid provided the cheapest footwear options, but boots and shoes made of these soon lost their shape, proving once again that you get what you pay for.

World War I brought with it a shortage of leather, resulting in a new vogue for cloth-topped shoes and boots, as well as a need for functional footwear and black mourning shoes. Shoes for half-mourning were produced in combinations of black and gray or black and white.

Ribbed black wool stocking c.1901. *Mobile Millinery Museum and Costume Archive*. $50-65.

This advertising studio photograph was likely used to promote gentlemen's footwear. Model Arthur Hillyer points to his shoes, which are of a different style than those worn by his older companion. *Ella Philip Collection, Mobile Millinery Museum and Costume Archive.*

In this photograph, model Arthur Hillyer's worn work-boots contrast sharply with his natty suit and bowler. Photo by *Underwood & Underwood*, Montreal, Quebec. *Ella Philip Collection, Mobile Millinery Museum and Costume Archive.*

This postcard from 1909 shows a young girl in white leather Mary Janes and an elaborate lace dress. *Mobile Millinery Museum and Costume Archive.*

In this photograph, model Arthur Hillyer's pointed toe lace-ups more appropriately complement his costume. *Ella Philip Collection, Mobile Millinery Museum and Costume Archive.*

MAY GOOD LUCK FLING HER OLD SHOE AT YOU, YOU, YOU.

1911 postcard showing an out-dated and worn-out shoe. *Mobile Millinery Museum and Costume Archive.*

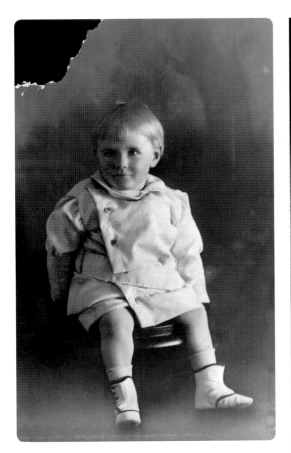

A young boy in button-closure boots with contrast binding. *Mobile Millinery Museum and Costume Archive.*

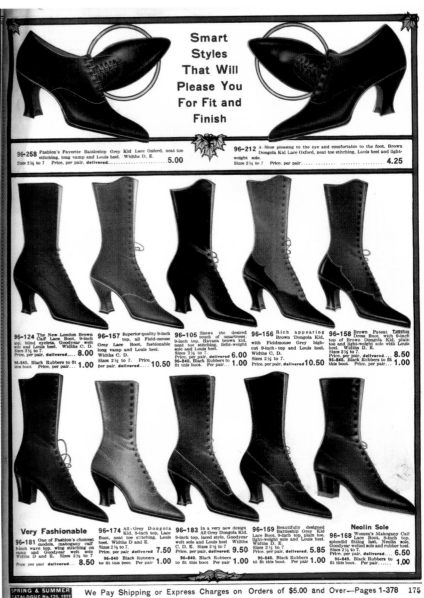

1919: Modish lace-up boots available to Canadian consumers through mail order. *Eaton's Spring & Summer Catalogue 1919. Courtesy of Ron Minaker.*

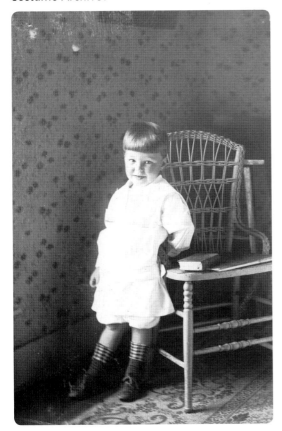

C.1914: A young boy in dark oxfords and ribbon-trimmed stockings. *Mobile Millinery Museum and Costume Archive.*

Mildred Philip's Edwardian costume rests above the ankle to reveal pretty white footwear with pointed toes. *Ella Philip Collection, Mobile Millinery Museum and Costume Archive.*

This family portrait c.1916 shows a woman whose skirt rises a hand's-length above the ankle to reveal her pointy-toed shoes. *Ella Philip Collection, Mobile Millinery Museum and Costume Archive.*

No. 102. One-Button Novelty Sack
Upper patch pocket
Lower circular pockets
Fancy sleeve cuffs
Stitched on belt in rear

This fashion plate from 1919, advertising a gentleman's suit model, also illustrates a woman's two-tone lace-up boots with Louis heel. *Mobile Millinery Museum and Costume Archive.*

Side button boots C.1910. *Courtesy of Jordan Museum.* A similar item might sell for $200-250.

The silhouette of 1919, shown with the delicate pointy-toed heels of the day. *Eaton's Spring & Summer Catalogue, 1919. Courtesy of Ron Minaker.*

C.1920: Ladies black and cream leather shoe with Art Deco detailing. Patent leather Louis heel, black leather insole. *Niagara Historical Society Museum.* Value undisclosed.

High-laced leather boot, worn by Mrs. S. H. Culp c.1900 to 1910. *Courtesy of Jordan Museum.* A similar item might sell for $250-300.

White kid wedding slipper, size 35-4. Worn by Austella Moyer at her marriage to Mr. Harry Couse, Sept. 29th, 1909. *Courtesy of Jordan Museum.* 580.42: A similar item might sell for $200-250.

1919: Ella Philip in black stockings and lace-ups entertains a friend whose feet are shod in smart black "Victory" pumps. *Ella Philip Collection, Mobile Millinery Museum and Costume Archive.*

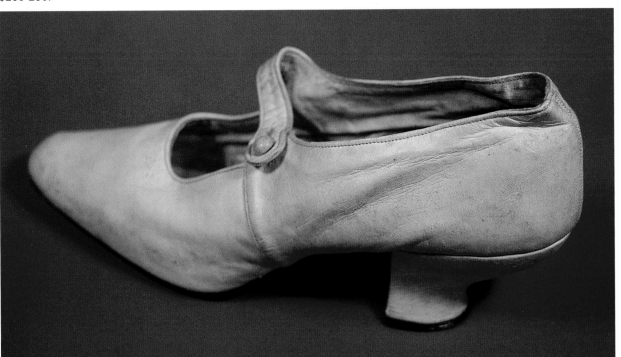

Gentlemen's rubber-soled slipper of discoloured red velvet. Rubber sole, banded, self-fabric tongue. "*Saika-voiva*" is written in ink on the inside. *Niagara Historical Society Museum.* Value undisclosed.

C.1916: Child's raspberry leather, 3-eyelet boot with ecru -coloured decorative stitching along tongue and nose. Label: "*So Easy*" printed on the inside. *Niagara Historical Society Museum.* Value undisclosed.

Chinese slippers of azure blue silk, faded to bronze. Toes are decorated with cream silk embroidery. Hand quilted soles, red fabric insoles. *Niagara Historical Society Museum.* Value undisclosed.

Detail showing original color.

Detail showing hand-tufted soles.

Girl's brown leather, ankle-strap boots bound in soft brown cotton. Single button closure, scalloped leather toe medallions. The brown leather soles are engraved with a maple twig motif. *Niagara Historical Society Museum.* Value undisclosed.

Pewter silk bar shoes c.1915, bound with ecru stitching Louis heel, pearl button closure. Partial maker's mark legible on insole: *"Flint Kent"*. *Niagara Historical Society Museum (Mrs. Calvin Rand).* Value undisclosed.

Child's grape-coloured metallic-sheen boot with 4-button closure. Red leather interior binding. "Size 3" stamped on interior. *Niagara Historical Society Museum.* Value undisclosed.

Beige, high-button boots, owned by film star Ann Harding. *Courtesy of Star Wares Collectibles & Larry's Shoe Museum.* $200-250.

Detail (interior).

Black leather walking shoe with sturdy block heel. *Mobile Millinery Museum and Costume Archive.* $75-175.

Girl's pink leather ankle-strap shoe with matching rosette (button missing). *Niagara Historical Society Museum.* Value undisclosed.

Chapter Three
Galoshes and Charleston Shoes:
1920-1930

The shoes worn today by the well dressed woman give the final touch of completeness and style. - Robert Simpson Spring & Summer Catalogue, 1921

I remember a craze for 'Russian Boots' in the twenties. They laced up the front and were trimmed with fur. We all wanted them. - Iris Hillyer

This "Shoes of To-day" advertisement features the ultra sleek "Victory pump". *Robert Simpson Catalogue, Spring and Summer 1921. Courtesy of Ron Minaker.*

With short hemlines, the proliferation of jazz, and the craze for dances such as the Charleston, the foot; and therefore the shoe, enjoyed a new fashion emphasis. Egyptian and art deco themes were developed on block and sturdy-but-high heels, while hand-painting, beading, and appliqués ornamented square toes. Metallic fabrics and diamanté trims were introduced; removable buckles and bows flourished, and stockings rolled down to reveal rouged, schoolgirl knees.

Glamorous, elevated sandals with waisted heels came into vogue for the first time, as the invention of the metal arch support eliminated the need for a toecap. On the heels of *World War I*, when pointed toes were still in vogue, the "Victory Pump", a long slender shoe with a Louis heel and a high Colonial tongue, was popular. Other styles, produced in gunmetal gray, also made reference to the war.

For a short time, leather dress boots and cloth-topped sport shoes held over from the previous decade.

Taps were developed for dance shoes in 1928, replacing what were formerly known as hard and soft shoes. T-straps, ankle-strap Mary Janes, and cut-away pumps fastened with a single, self-fabric shoe button or buckle fastenette.

As the price of rubber tumbled in 1921 through 1924, to less than half of what it had been in 1917, and half of what it would be again by 1925, the use of this newly-inexpensive material for footwear, increased. Wedge-heeled, rubber bathing shoes and resort sandals turned up at the beach, and rubber overshoes patrolled the streets. Galoshes became so popular that some designers offered a boot-back, open-fronted shoe. *Eaton's Department Store* termed their version of this hybrid, c.1929, the "Miss Billy-Boy." A fad for wearing unbuckled galoshes developed among young women of the 1920s. Those who scoffed at prohibition could slide a flask into the open boot.

By 1929, spike heels supported round-toed "1-straps" in fabric and patent leather. Less dainty but equally stylish triple-eyelet lace-ups, offered in reptile and reptile-finish leather, rested on Cuban heels. Black, brown, and white-kid were seen more often than the earlier navy and gray tones, but a caramel-toned shade named "sunburn" became the new rage. Gold and silver-kid Charleston shoes dominated at night.

Black stockings were forsaken for flesh-colored silk hose for evening, while patterned stockings of cotton and wool accessorized daytime leisurewear.

1921: These images of women's dress shoes illustrate the pointed toes, low heels and steel buckles popular at the outset of the decade. *Robert Simpson Catalogue, Spring and Summer 1921. Courtesy of Ron Minaker*.

1926: This woman's shoes boast prominent buckles. *Ella Philip Collection*, *Mobile Millinery Museum and Costume Archive*.

Men's dress shoe advertisement, 1921. *Robert Simpson Catalogue, Spring and Summer 1921. Courtesy of Ron Minaker.*

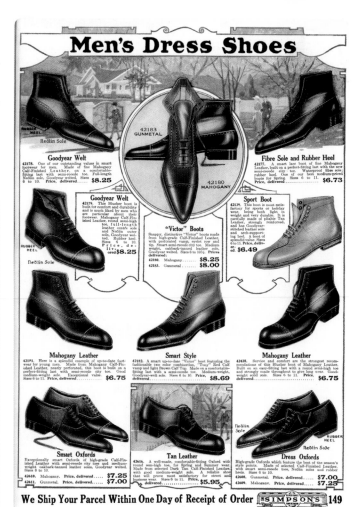

'Play and Dress footwear": Shoe styles for children and young girls c.1921. *Robert Simpson Catalogue, Spring and Summer 1921. Courtesy of Ron Minaker.*

Men's stylish work boots advertised in 1921. *Robert Simpson Catalogue, Spring and Summer 1921. Courtesy of Ron Minaker.*

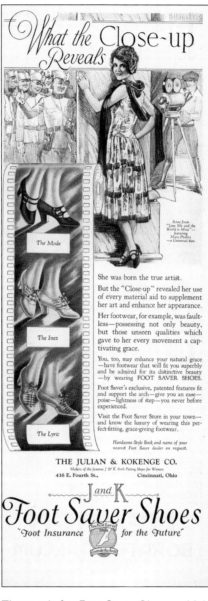

This ad for *McCallum* hosiery which appeared in the February, 1927 issue of *The Ladies' Home Journal,* nicely illustrates the shoes of the day as well as the skirt length and hosiery they were designed to accessorize. *Mobile Millinery Museum and Costume Archive.*

These ads for *Foot Saver Shoes*, which appeared in the March and May issues of *The Ladies Home Journal,* utilize sketches of and references to, film stars, to sell their footwear named *"The Trudie"*, *"The Mode"*, *"The Inez"*, and *"The Lyric"*. *Mobile Millinery Museum and Costume Archive.*

The *Irving Drew Company* emphasised comfort through arch support in their full-page ad, which appeared in the May, 1927 issue of *The Ladies' Home Journal. Mobile Millinery Museum and Costume Archive.*

This infant poses for his portrait in two-tone leather booties. *Mobile Millinery Museum and Costume Archive.*

A young boy in leather shoes and patterned stockings. *Jane Thomas Collection, Mobile Millinery Museum and Costume Archive.*

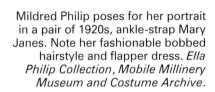

Mildred Philip poses for her portrait in a pair of 1920s, ankle-strap Mary Janes. Note her fashionable bobbed hairstyle and flapper dress. *Ella Philip Collection, Mobile Millinery Museum and Costume Archive.*

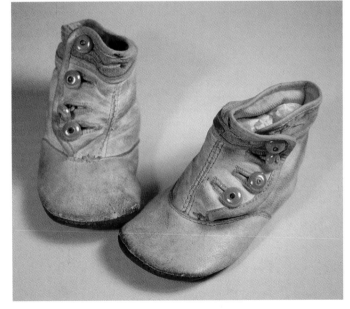

1921: A child's white leather booties with canvas interior. Brown leather soles. Worn by Alexander MacIntyre. *Mobile Millinery Museum and Costume Archive.* $85-125.

1920s suede and leather ankle-cuff bootie reveals an Art Deco influence. Label: *T. Eaton Co. Ltd. Aline Banting Collection, Mobile Millinery Museum and Costume Archive.* $300-350.

Brown suede, punch-cut bar shoes worn by Charlotte Robins. *Courtesy of Marilyn Bumstead.* $125-150.

Open-toed gold kid Charleston shoe. Leather insole. These shoes have been handed down through four generations and have recently passed from grandmother to granddaughter as an engagement gift. *Courtesy of Kathryn Crowder.* A similar item might sell for $250-325.

1929: Iris Thomas in fashionable winter attire. Note the slip-on boots. *Mobile Millinery Museum and Costume Archive.*

View showing decorative heel.

C.1920: Bronze satin dance shoes with mother-of-pearl button closure. Cream leather insoles. Label: "*Hickley's* hand turns, narrow heel " (stamped on insole), "custom made" (stamped on sole). *Niagara Historical Society Museum.* Value undisclosed.

These satin-bound powder-pink slippers have never been worn. *Aline Banting Collection, Mobile Millinery Museum and Costume Archive.* $300-375.

Ladies ankle strap of gray-blue leather with rectangular decorative inserts and 2-button closure. 2-inch Louis heel. *"Paris 1925"* is handwritten on each sole. Label: *Chaussures Raoul*, Paris. 17B rue de la Madeleine". French soldier Roger Trentesaux remembered passing the *Raoul Shoe Store* and seeing its windows blown out during the liberation of Paris in 1944. *Niagara Historical Society Museum.* Value undisclosed.

Silver kid Charleston shoe. Taupe leather insole. Label: Made Expressly for *Simpson's. Aline Banting Collection, Mobile Millinery Museum and Costume Archive.* $250-325.

Detail.

Silver kid, t-strap Charleston shoe. Open-toe, white leather insole. *Aline Banting Collection, Mobile Millinery Museum and Costume Archive*. $250-325.

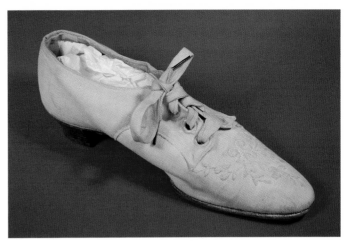

C.1920: Ladies white canvas oxfords with embroidered toes. *Courtesy of Jordan Museum.* A similar item might sell on the retail market for $200-250.

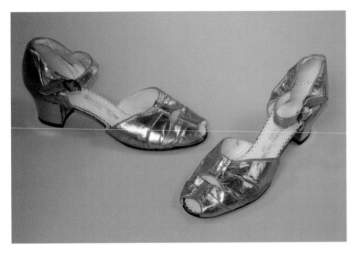

Late 1920s Charleston shoe. Overlapping bows of gold kid allow a peek at the toes. White leather insole boasts a scalloped edge. Label: *Fitzgerald Shoe Shop*, Chatham, On. $200-250.

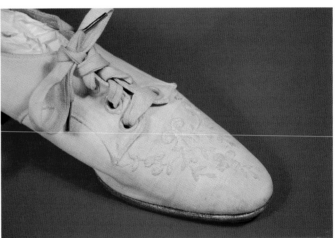

Detail.

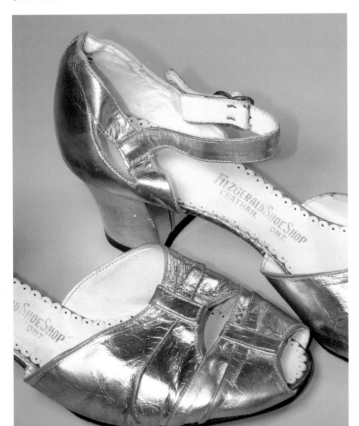

Pink and black satin, *Daniel Green* slippers from actress Gloria Swanson's personal collection. Faded peach satin lining, peach silk floral adornment. Patterned silk toe pads. $755. *Courtesy of Star Wares Collectibles & Larry's Shoe Museum.* $755.

Detail.

Chapter Four
The Swagger Years: 1930-1940

I knew a man, Bojangles and he danced for you
In worn out shoes
Silver hair, a ragged shirt and baggy pants
The old soft shoe - From *Mr. Bojangles* by Jerry Jeff Walker

My Christmas brother's gift to me was always $10, which I quickly spent
at the fancy shoe stores in downtown Toronto. - Nora Robinson, *"Shoe*
and Tell" attendee.

During the Depression, a desire for escapism brought new emphasis to the silver screen and to the fashions portrayed there. Lengthened hemvlines required that camera shots include the feet of actors and actresses, shod in footwear the public would soon imitate. Buyers responded to advertising copy that suggested a diversion from economic woes. Magazines and catalogues carried shoe sketches alongside tag lines like "snap and dash", "endorsed by Dame Fashion", and "suggesting the gay witchery of a summer day".

Madeleine Vionett's invention of the bias-cut enabled dressmakers to create gowns with elasticity and cling, ideal for dancing. During the evening, flared and handkerchief hemlines rested above the ankle to show off round-toed pumps with high vamps, while daywear required a more masculine shoe in keeping with the wide-legged trousers, beach pyjamas, and scandalous new shorts of the decade.

More and more, buckles replaced buttons on bar and t-strap dress shoes, even as two-eyelet ties in suede and calf combinations prevailed for daywear. By 1933, three-button, strapped shoes, while still available, were subtly marketed to out-of-date matrons. One pair, offered in *Eaton's* catalogue for nearly double the price of patent leather pumps, boasted "extra room for enlarged joints or bunions." The style went by the name "Aunt Mary."

On the street and at the office, pumps gained popularity over lace-ups; although, bow-trimmed, low-heeled dress shoes and ribbon-tied bluchers were offered for comfort. T-strap fabric sandals with covered Cuban heels, kept toes cool in summer through mesh vamps or braided leather. These were offered in white, blue, tan, and awning stripe. Colored leather shoes first introduced by designer Dan Palter, gained widespread approval.

The arch of the foot was emphasized through decorative (sometimes twin) tongues and center-buckle straps. Ribbon trims and top-stitching competed with pin-dots and punched leather for eye appeal. Tanned feet and painted toenails were exposed in strappy sandals and open-toed pumps. The peep-toes, designed by Dan Palter and first marketed at *Palter-Deliso,* shocked the shoe-buying public at first, but by 1936 even Queen Elizabeth, wife of Britain's King George VI, was enchanted by them; so much so, that she commissioned Perugia to make her a pair for a state visit to Paris.

Ladies' house shoes in combinations of leather and canvas or velveteen, sold for half the price of dress shoes, but slightly more than the cost of leather slippers. High-cut lace-ups described as "neat" and "comfortable" served as work boots, for women laboring "around the house and outdoors."

By mid-decade, designers produced sober, round-toed pumps with high vamps that covered the instep, to complement the longer, bias-cut dresses which had replaced the flapper silhouette. Thick 3-inch heels were referred to as "spikes".

By 1938, the most fashionable laced day shoes sported enlarged "wedding ring" or "balloon" eyelets. These sold for five to ten dollars per pair. That same year, slender-heeled evening slippers of gold or silver fabric, cut low on the sides to reveal the instep, could be purchased for $2.79. In some cases that price included mail delivery charges.

Dual-color correspondent shoes reached the height of fashion by 1939.

Flat-heeled calfskin and patent leather shoes for girls imitated those designed for women, and carried names like "the Peasant Shoe", "the Swagger", and "the Shawl-tongued Oxford". Some children's shoes c.1935, were packed in little green suitcases which proud owners used to carry doll clothes or school lunches.

Rubber prices slumped even further with new lows achieved c.1932-1933. The footwear industry with access to this inexpensive, malleable raw material, responded by producing rubber overshoes.

These were molded to fit over flat and Cuban-heeled dress shoes, or fashioned as knee-high "rubbers". Dome fasteners allowed for crossover closure, and ladies' boot styles returned to a sleek silhouette.

Throughout the decade, ladies wore silk hose or seamed stockings of a wool/rayon blend. In foul weather, thigh-high, wool "sloshers" protected legs and stockings from slush and mud. Children wore ribbed stockings of cotton and/or wool and cashmere in a variety of colors. Consumers prolonged the life of their leather footwear with shoe coloring and applied less expensive "*Shu Milk*" to white canvas styles.

These seven pages *(shown here and on the following page)* from the *Eaton's* Catalogue for 1932 and 1933 depict Canadian shoe styles and prices for women and children. *Courtesy of Ron Minaker.*

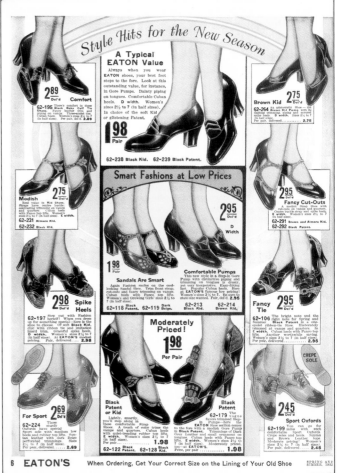

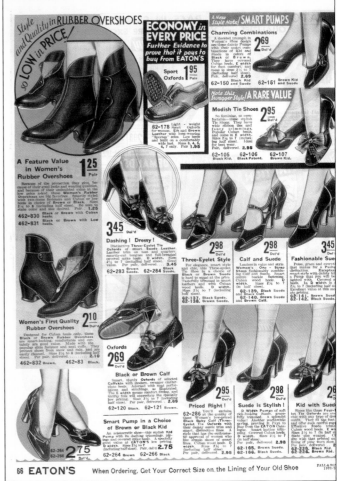

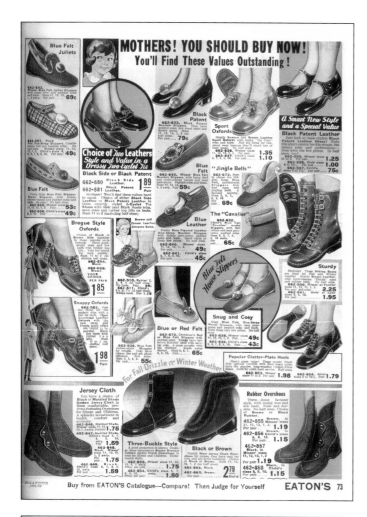

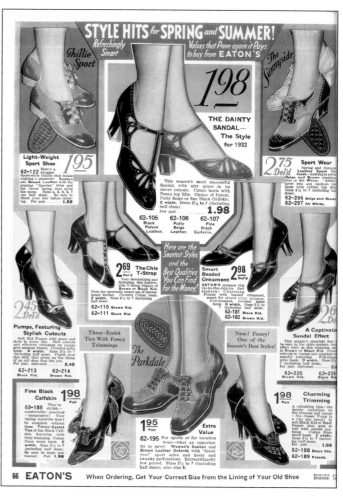

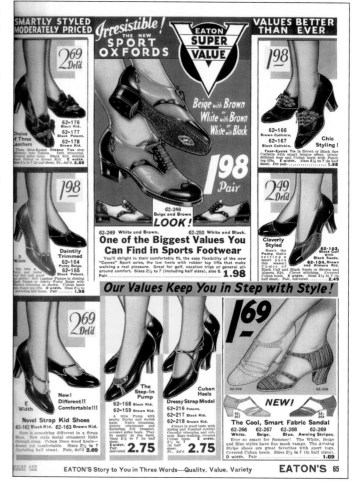

54

This photograph taken outside of *Simpson's Department Store* c.1939, depicts a group of shoppers taking long strides in their low-heeled walking shoes. *Mobile Millinery Museum and Costume Archive*.

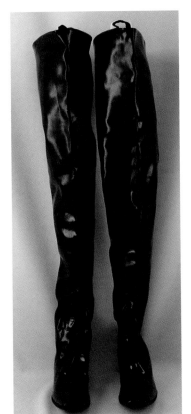

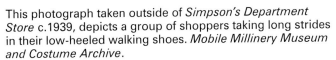

Kathleen O'Brien perches on a bridge in fashionable tie and trousers to show off her two-toned oxfords. *Courtesy of Iris Hillyer*.

Navy and white punch-cut leather peep-toes with Cuban heel and bow trim. *Emily Ruth Peircy Collection, Mobile Millinery Museum and Costume Archive*. $60-80.

Ginger Rogers' black rubber, thigh-high, leg-hugging boots. Size: 7½. *Courtesy of Star Wares Collectibles & Larry's Shoe Museum*. Value undisclosed.

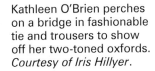

Gray silk decorated pump with 2½-inch boulevard heel. Label: *Foot Delight Shoes*, Made in U.S.A. *Aline Banting Collection, Mobile Millinery Museum and Costume Archive*. $120-150.

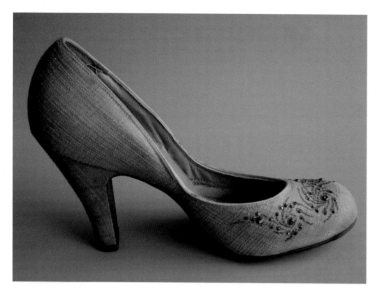

A similar shoe in gold textured silk with painted, jewelled-toe detail. Beige leather insoles, 3-inch wooden heel. *Aline Banting Collection, Mobile Millinery Museum and Costume Archive.* $140-160.

Detail.

Cream silk pumps appliquéd at the toe with cream and brown cording. *Aline Banting Collection, Mobile Millinery Museum and Costume Archive.* $100-120.

C.1932: An early rubber overshoe fits glove-like, over a pair of Cuban-heeled walking shoes. *Aline Banting Collection, Mobile Millinery Museum and Costume Archive.* $35-55.

C.1935: Punch-cut, purple suede peep-toe with criss-cross straps and two-tone gray leather insole. *Niagara Historical Society Museum (Anne Buyers).* Value undisclosed.

C. 1938: This white leather and navy suede shoe with its bold stripes and wedding ring eyelets holds special appeal. Gray leather insole, 2-inch heel. *Aline Banting Collection, Mobile Millinery Museum and Costume Archive.* $250-325.

These much-loved, blue leather, cutaways feature grosgrain trim. Bone leather insoles. Label: *Shoe of the Hour*. Made expressly for the *T. Eaton Co*. of Canada. Wooden, boulevard heels. *Mobile Millinery Museum and Costume Archive.* $75-125.

The brown striping on these sand-colored linen pumps emphasises the baby doll toes. Boulevard heels, leather insoles. Label: *Golden Pheasant. Aline Banting Collection, Mobile Millinery Museum and Costume Archive.* $75-125.

Cutwork lace-ups of chocolate brown suede. Brown leather insoles, wooden, boulevard heels. *Mobile Millinery Museum and Costume Archive.* $80-120.

An exquisitely shaped open-toed pump of vivid green leather. 2¾-inch wooden heel. Label: *Golden Pheasant*. *Aline Banting Collection, Mobile Millinery Museum and Costume Archive.* $200-250.

Beautifully shaped peep-toes in ash gray suede. 2½-inch wooden heels. Label: *Exclusively for the Right House*, Hand Made. *Aline Banting Collection, Mobile Millinery Museum and Costume Archive.* $200-250.

Deep green suede pump with 2-inch heel. Green leather insole. Label: *Bachelor Girl*. *Aline Banting Collection, Mobile Millinery Museum and Costume Archive.* $125-150.

Sensational baby doll evening pumps. *Aline Banting Collection, Mobile Millinery Museum and Costume Archive.* $175-250.

Black suede baby dolls, top-stitched to add charm. Label: *Gold Cross Shoes. Aline Banting Collection, Mobile Millinery Museum and Costume Archive.* $50-75.

Black suede ankle boot with red leather trim. Black leather interior, 2¼-inch heel. Label: *Topper,* Hand Made. *Aline Banting Collection, Mobile Millinery Museum and Costume Archive.* $150-225.

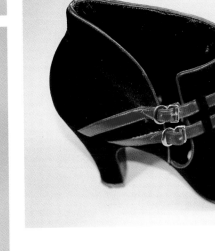

Detail.

This black satin cutaway hints at toe cleavage. Heel and toe of suede. 2½-inch boulevard heel, dainty, off-centre bow. Label: *Golden Pheasant*, Made in Canada. *Aline Banting Collection, Mobile Millinery Museum and Costume Archive.* $75-125.

Detail.

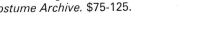

A sturdy, ankle-strap sandal, suitable for dancing. Label: *Bachelor Girl. Aline Banting Collection, Mobile Millinery Museum and Costume Archive.* $75-125.

More foot delight! The toes of these navy silk pumps are hand painted in a starburst motif with seed beads and rhinestones. 2½ heels, grosgrain top-line. Label: *Foot Delight Shoes*, Made in U.S.A. *Aline Banting Collection, Mobile Millinery Museum and Costume Archive.* $120-150.

Black leather pump with 2½-inch heel. Gray leather insole. Label: *Golden Pheasant*, Made in Canada. *Aline Banting Collection, Mobile Millinery Museum and Costume Archive.* $60-80.

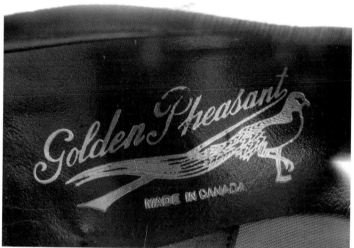

Detail.

Detail.

Detail.

Snakeskin pumps with 3½-inch heels, low-walled to accentuate the instep. Label: *Hand Fashioned Shoes,* Made in USA. *Emily Ruth Peircy Collection, Mobile Millinery Museum and Costume Archive.* $150-175.

This boot box provides instructions for its conversion to a shoe carrier; the bottom can be cut and folded to become a cord-handled case. *Aline Banting Collection, Mobile Millinery Museum and Costume Archive.* $18-25.

Clark Gable's suede, wing-tip oxfords. Size 12. Maker: *Carroll & Co. Courtesy of Star Wares Collectibles & Larry's Shoe Museum.* Value undisclosed.

Size 12, brown leather wingtips from the personal collection of actor Errol Flynn. Label: *Stacy Adams. Courtesy of Star Wares Collectibles & Larry's Shoe Museum.* Value undisclosed.

Fred Astaire's handsewn, white oxford rehearsal shoe. Label: *I. Miller. Courtesy of Star Wares Collectibles & Larry's Shoe Museum.* Value undisclosed.

Brown leather lace-ups, owned by Judy Garland and shown with her publicity photo. Child's size: 11½C. Label: Judy's name is printed on the inside of the shoes. *Courtesy of Star Wares Collectibles & Larry's Shoe Museum.* Value undisclosed.

Chapter Five
Platforms and Yankee-Catchers: 1940-1950

When I was in the air force I discovered a little secret to giving my ox-fords that extra-special shine for parade days. At the end of my polishing routine, I spit on my shoe and rubbed with the vigour of a shoeshine boy until I felt warmth on my foot. No parade sergeant ever complained about my shoes. - Marie Minaker

With the advent of the Second World War, government restrictions were placed on the fashion industry in regard to leather items, and the embellishment of clothing and footwear; "Utility" styles appeared in response to design regulations, and rationing guidelines were published in newspapers and magazines, clearly explaining procedures and ticket allotments. In Britain in 1941; for example, five ration tickets were required for the purchase of a pair of women's boots or shoes. Ration books of sixty-six coupons were to last the year. America instituted a similar program in 1942.

Elasticized gores and vamps replaced lacings and buckles on ladies shoes in 1940 and obscure terms like "simulated frog-skin" were used to describe inferior grades of leather. A fresh silhouette appeared as designers offered buyers the new snub-nose "curbstone toe" and high-walled last, which promised to make feet look smaller. "Trig" bows made subtle reference to patriotism, and the Cuban heel was replaced by a medium block support referred to as the military heel.

By 1941, natural materials, including leather, were commandeered for the war effort, leaving shoe designers to experiment with alternatives such as wood, cork, mesh, and reptile skin. Manufacturers also made use of remnants by combining faux-patent with suede for street wear. Cotton and wool were reserved for slippers while velvet ankle boots with fur trim and quilted linings served as "Motor Boots."

Wooden clogs could be freely purchased without ration tickets, and corked heels appeared on wedgies c.1942. A hollowed variation of the wedge called the "sled heel" was experimented with briefly. Manufacturers produced low-cut, plain black rubbers styled to fit a variety of women's shoe styles. They sold for fifty-three cents per pair. These could be worn with cotton shoe protectors, which sold for twenty-five cents per pair.

Children and teens found comfort and durability in rubber-soled saddle shoes in brown, blue, white, and tan, as color range was restricted by the government.

Traditional heels diminished in height. In an article on women's military uniforms in the April 1941 issue of Canada's *Chatelaine Magazine*, Norma Gibb credits the "comfort and support of low-heeled shoes" with straightening backs and improving posture.

During the war, embellishment was left to the individual consumer, with magazines offering tips on recycling household items like pipe cleaners and cellophane to create decorations. Peep-toe shoes disappeared until after the conflict as they were considered frivolous and unsafe for the factory-work that engaged so many women.

With silk stockings in short supply, the 1941 *Eaton's* catalogue presented nylon stockings as "test-tube hosiery" and promised they would not run. An inferior grade at half the price was termed "service chiffon". Heavy cotton and wool stockings were marketed for winter wear along with sloshers, which now featured stirrups.

By 1943, with North America no longer importing silk, and nylon performing full-time war work, rayon stockings were introduced (along with laundering instructions for extending their life, as the fibres weakened when exposed to perspiration and lost strength when wet). Many women painted their legs with gravy browning or make-up, and went barelegged, after drawing false seams on the backs of their legs with eyebrow pencil. Children and teens teamed their shoes with ankle socks, often hand-knit.

Following the war, heel heights increased and high-arched step-ins, embellished with butterfly bows or cut to reveal painted toes, proved popular. By the summer of 1947, open-heeled shoes were firmly established, many made from colourful "shoe cloth" which also covered heels and soles. The ankle-strap ring also made an appearance, promising to give ladies "that tall look". Crepe soles, of softer more flexible rubber, offered a springier step, and spectator pumps remained fashionable for all age groups. Nail-

Candy-apple red, high-arched, leather step-ins. Black elastic top-line. Narrow black cording ornaments the toes. 3-inch heels. Label: *Shalimar. Aline Banting Collection, Mobile Millinery Museum and Costume Archive.* $120-150.

Detail.

Label (cut into cream leather insole).

head trims competed with moccasin-style lacings as adornment. Shoe clips, configured as large leather, or plastic, bows and pompoms, ensured a multiplicity of looks with a single pair of shoes. Sombrero-motif appliqués adorned one style, which was marketed to complement a "Mexicana-brimmed" dress-hat in the *Eaton's* catalogue. Rayon stockings now available without seams, were still in short supply and offered "one only per customer" in many locations. *Eaton's* catalogue boasted that Canadian women accepted the less expensive, more accessible, cotton lisle hose, which featured a ribbed, elasticized band.

At the close of the decade, higher heels aligned with longer skirts to produce a tall silhouette. Low-cut, snub-nose pumps, many with novelty throat-lines, carried names like "snubbies" and the "baby doll," while advertisements promised casual summer shoes in "dagger-bright" colors. Unique footwear began to appear; in fact, one particular style incorporated a lipstick tube in the heel, reflecting the lighter spirits of the postwar era. Sling-backs in plastic, made-to-look-like-python, dared to be seen. Warm weather "strap slippers" boasted of "airy foot-free fashion" while concealed elastic gores, added a new dimension to perky pumps.

Rita Hayworth's black suede, ankle-strap, platform pumps, shown with beige silk evening bag and publicity photo. Hand-made shoes are beaded. Label: *Marchioness*. "R.H." is printed on the bottom of the right shoe. Purse contains a white linen handkerchief monogrammed with an embroidered "R" and is marked *"Columbia Pictures* – R. Hayworth". *Courtesy of Star Wares Collectibles & Larry's Shoe Museum.* Value undisclosed.

Jayne Mansfield's tortoiseshell, platform slides, shown with cigarette case, cigarette holder, bakelite purse and publicity photo. *Courtesy of Star Wares Collectibles & Larry's Shoe Museum.* Value undisclosed.

C.1940: The shiny, thigh-hugging military boots worn by Major Charlie MacLean of the *Royal Canadian Hussars* give emphasis to the cut of the officer's jodhpurs. *Laurabelle MacLean Collection, Mobile Millinery Museum and Costume Archive.*

C.1948: This silver opalescent shoes/handbag/cosmetic bag ensemble is a fine example of the many plastic and plastic-encased accessory items, custom-made for Joan Crawford. Roslyn Herman of *Roslyn Herman & Co.,* reports that Joan was uncomfortable when asked to perform in close-toe shoes due to her belief that her feet should be aired. Label: *Leach-Kale Shoes. Courtesy of Star Wares Collectibles & Larry's Shoe Museum.* Value undisclosed.

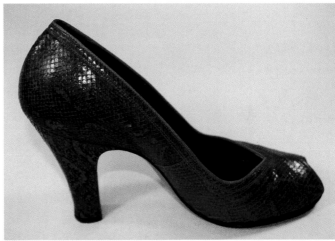

A high-arched, red snakeskin step-in. A vee-shaped peep-toe mirrors the v-cut throat. Grosgrain binding, 3-inch heel, brown leather insole. *Aline Banting Collection, Mobile Millinery Museum and Costume Archive.* $150-200.

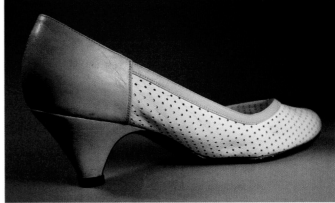

Two-toned peep-toe in flesh and white, punch-cut leather, 2-inch Cuban heel. Label: *Thomas Wallace. Emily Ruth Peircy Collection, Mobile Millinery Museum and Costume Archive.* $60-80.

C.1940: This photograph shows Kathleen O'Brien in a pair of suede shoes with criss-cross straps while her Aunt Jane wears a pair of $8.00 *"Aunt Mary Ties"*. *Mobile Millinery Museum and Costume Archive.*

Red-seamed stockings with French heels. *Mobile Millinery Museum and Costume Archive*. $35-50.

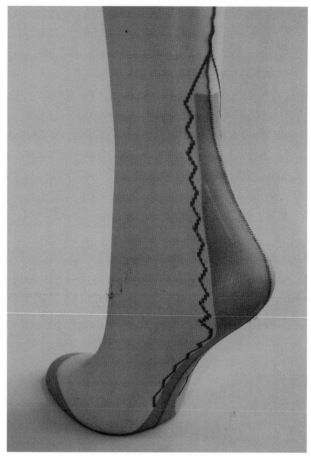

Detail.

Silver "shoe-cloth" sling-backs with wedge heels. Velveteen insoles. *Mobile Millinery Museum and Costume Archive*. $75-100.

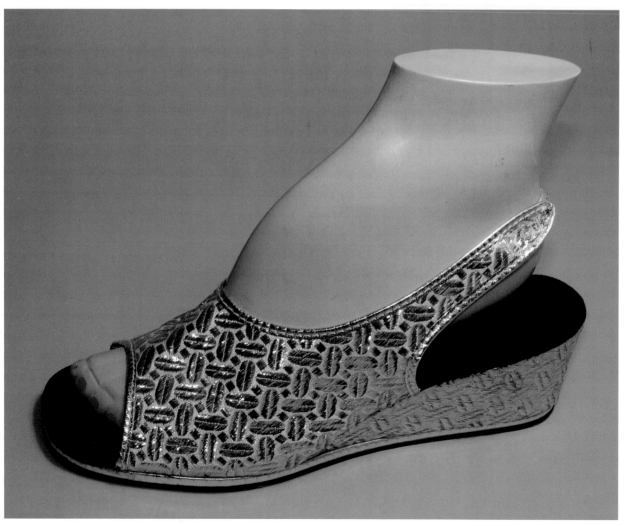

This reptile-look 1940s platform shoe was known in Canada as a *"Yankee Catcher"*. 3-inch heel, gray leather insole, Label: *T. Eaton Co. Ltd.*, Canada. *Aline Banting Collection, Mobile Millinery Museum and Costume Archive.* $120-150.

Pink leather peep-toe snubbies with beaded toe adornment. Label: Made in Switzerland*, Bally* - Paris, New York. *Aline Banting Collection, Mobile Millinery Museum and Costume Archive.* $60-80.

A second *"Yankee Catcher"*: Ankle strap platform of suede and reptile skin. Leather insole. Label: *Golden Pheasant*. *Aline Banting Collection, Mobile Millinery Museum and Costume Archive.* $150-200.

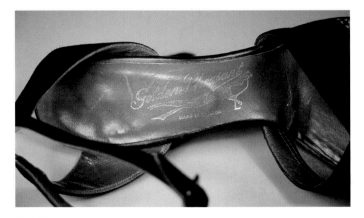

Detail.

Detail: The identical shoe in gray-blue. Label: *Arlette, The T. Eaton Co. Ltd.,* Made in Switzerland. 2-inch heels. *Aline Banting Collection, Mobile Millinery Museum and Costume Archive.* $60-80.

A sturdy, reptile-skin platform shoe. Label: *Pedulla &
Agostino Limited, Mode Art. Aline Banting Collection, Mobile
Millinery Museum and Costume Archive.* $150-200.

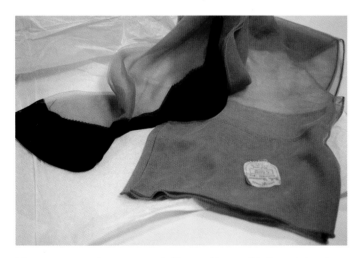

These navy and tan seamed silk stockings with French heels,
were never worn but preserved in their original gift box with
a card which reads "To Margaret, From George J." *Mobile
Millinery Museum and Costume Archive.* $40-50.

These three-fingered mitts were worn to prevent snags when
pulling on stockings. *Mobile Millinery Museum and Costume
Archive.* $30-40.